THE
VISITATION

An
Archangel's
Prophecy

Mary Summer Rain

D0029501

HAMPTON ROADS
PUBLISHING COMPANY, INC.

For information write:

Hampton Roads Publishing Company, Inc.
134 Burgess Lane
Charlottesville, VA 22902

Or call: (804) 296-2772
FAX: (804) 296-5096
e-mail: hrpc@mail.hrpub.com
Internet: http://www.hrpub.com

If you are unable to order this book from your local
bookseller, you may order directly from the publisher.
Quantity discounts for organizations are available.
Call 1-800-766-8009, toll-free.

ISBN 1-57174-062-7

10 9 8 7 6 5 4 3 2 1

Printed on acid-free paper in the United States of America

I am sitting at a kitchen table writing by oil lamp in the middle of a snowy December night, and in fourteen days it will be Christmas of 1996.

All is silent save the heartbeat ticking of the Black Forest clock in the living room and the occasional howling and yipping of the coyote pack as it passes by this cabin tucked between aspen, spruce, and pine.

The cabin, a modest two-bedroom cedar place, rests atop a valley ridge at 10,000 feet in the Colorado Rockies. It is remote enough to have no electricity and is heated solely by the crackling fire of an old woodstove.

This place signifies a new start for me, one that marks a transitional stage and has bestowed blessings of a peaceful heart and a deep tranquility of being I've never known before. It's given me a total inner calm that comes with the complete acceptance of that which came before. It has bestowed upon me a childlike wonder over experiencing each new sunrise, as more than a thousand rosy finches gather in the winter-bare aspens to anxiously watch me fill the floor of my covered porch with their breakfast seed. Silently, I sit on the cypress rocker to share in their joy as they flock down to feast at my feet. The sight is an amazement and, at first, I can't contain some giggles, but then I calm to the broad smile that a full heart brings. I thank God for the blessings of the beautiful sanctuary that brought me to this serene state of being.

Yet all was not so wonderful a mere six months ago when I lived in a three-room cabin and my life had been torn asunder so completely that nothing had rhyme or reason to it anymore. It was there where my inner strength was put to the ultimate test — and survived. It was there where my future path was defined while I prayed my heart out in the night woods. It was there where a personal guardian was sent to me. And it was there where an archangel of the Lord made a visitation upon me.

SIX MONTHS EARLIER

The small three-room cabin was more like a country cottage made of stone and snugly nestled into the earth on three sides. Surrounded by forest, it was a refuge from the three years of personal turmoil I was attempting to deal with and heal from. I was deep in the difficult and complex process of overcoming the painful feeling of being tossed aside — thrown away — by those I loved and who I believed loved me. I was trying to rid myself of the hurt of the Self and simply accept how others around me behaved. Inch by painful inch I was gaining ground and I would've been all alone in my efforts had it not been for a very special individual who was sent to help see me through this most traumatic time of transition. Sally felt like an angel sent by the Powers That Be to be my grounding force; my helper, guardian, and friend.

Meanwhile, I kept centered on trying to accept the fact that no amount of rational deductions could explain the illogical words and actions of those close to me and I eventually concluded that my efforts to gain rationale were frustratingly futile. I was working hard on just plain dealing — dealing with it all and not allowing the heart of a wife and mother to be seared beyond function. I realized that personal heart pain was a choice; it was a choice either to nurture or release and, inch by inch, I was letting it drop away into my past instead of holding onto it. I was healing, and healing time required my full attention and rest; therefore, I took a break from writing and was planning to sell my little stone cabin next spring to shed the final remnants of bad memories it carried. I was holding my own when, one sunny June afternoon, my real estate friend, Jane, called.

"I found the place you've always looked for. Want to see it?"

I was so taken off guard I didn't know how to respond. Silence hung between us while a zillion thoughts sped through my mind. I was trying to settle my husband's estate by selling our former house — and it *wasn't* selling. I was having difficulty keeping up on my own cabin payments. I was dealing with too much and trying to rest and heal. I had no money to buy a place even if I loved it. This was nuts. Just nuts.

"Don't tease me, Jane, it's not feasible, and besides, I am dealing with too much right now." The thought of packing up and moving was overwhelming to me. I was just not ready to tackle that kind of activity at that time.

After I hung up, my friend and I talked it over. In her impeccable logic she wisely reminded me of Destiny and how things could work out if they truly were meant to be.

Well yes, I knew that, but the current situation with the estate house sitting empty on the market for so long, having no funds for a down payment, then having to sell the cabin on top of it — it was just too complex to expect everything to come together. I saw it as a minute probability and a huge long shot. To my way of thinking, it was pure insanity to think there was even the slightest of possibilities that such an involved set of technicalities could meld into a fruitful outcome.

My companion posed a question after I'd finished expressing my viewpoint to her. "What if this place Jane has is meant for you? What if it's your final place of rest after all you've been through? Don't you think you ought to at least look at it?"

I was thinking.

She continued. "You've been through hell. You've been down to less than a hundred pounds and are coming back up with your healing. I see so many aspects of your life as ending and, with endings come beginnings. What do you have to lose by just looking at this place? And what if it is where your Advisors want you to be? What then?"

What then? Would they really load me down with this kind of activity while I was working so hard on healing? And I asked that question of my friend. Her response was logical.

"I see you sitting and moping, remembering too many painful events, still attempting to find a shred of reason for all that's happened." She sighed. "Yet all that comes out of it is frustration as you mentally go around and around with it. Mary, if this other place is meant for you it will mean that your Advisors see a therapeutic means to help you heal quicker. Packing and moving will give you something to *do*! It'll get your mind on other things."

Well that was certainly true, I thought.

Now I sighed. "Still, with no way to buy it? Isn't that kind of like having a kid look through a candy store window then say she can't have any?"

"You don't know that yet. If it's meant for you. . .it'll happen."

I was not that easily swayed. "I've no down payment."

"You've got enough to put earnest money down on an offer," came her surprising reply.

"I don't do business that way. How could I make an offer knowing I don't have the backup funds to carry the deal through?"

Sally shook her head. "I've got an idea. I could borrow the down from Mary Belle (her mother) and then, when the cabin sells, we can pay her right back."

"When the *cabin* sells! It's not even for sale yet!" I was used to factoring in all foreseeable probabilities to a plan.

"Oh for Pete's sake!" she exclaimed in growing frustration. "Let's just go see if Jane knows you well enough to know what she's talking about. Maybe this isn't what you want and all this finagling will be a moot point anyway."

I relented and Jane took us out. It wasn't a moot point. It was exactly what I'd spent twenty years searching for. It even overlooked a valley that had always pulled at my heart every time I drove by it.

We turned into a forest and wove our way through pine, spruce, and quaking aspen for a quarter mile. That was the driveway. We ended at a cedar-sided place that overlooked the picture-perfect valley. Springs. Aspen and pine. And though over fourteen years old, the cabin had never been lived in. It had been a weekend do-it-yourself project for the two former owners. When we walked inside we were greeted by plywood floors and sheetrock on all the walls. No bathroom sink. No electricity. A weather-worn platform marked where a deck was planned. A covered front porch with log rails that looked out upon the virgin valley where the sunset would gild it gold. Yet there was enough tongue-in-groove knotty pine paneling stacked in the basement to finish off the entire interior.

I fell in love with it. Jane knew me well. It was me.

To make a long story short, my friend did borrow the down payment from her mother and Jane called me the following day with an offer on the estate house. Two days after that she called again.

"I have someone here who wants to see your cabin."

My skin prickled. "It's not even for sale yet!"

She had a big smile in her voice. "That estate house sat for months and months with no interest in it and now we have an offer that looks good. You want to buy that unfinished cabin and now it looks like your cabin could sell quick. Looks to me like *somebody* upstairs is pulling some strings to get you into that other place."

Her interested party came out that evening to look over my stone cabin and wrote an offer that night, before the listing papers were even drawn up. My companion had taught me a good lesson in having faith in my Advisors and how easily they can handle earthly technicalities that appear impossible to us humans. Indeed, Destiny had laid out a path and taken care of all the problematical facets while all I had to do was follow the glowing bread crumbs dropped along the way.

While waiting for the paperwork to process on all three houses I diligently continued to accept, rest, and heal. These were facilitated by my walks in the woods, packing up the cabin, and daily periods of extended meditation time while my companion handled all the worldly aspects of our life such as business calls, grocery shopping, and routine chores such as splitting wood and hauling in food for the deer and birds.

One evening, while deep into an extended meditation beside the snapping fire of the cabin woodstove, a brilliant light appeared beyond my closed eyelids. I opened them to behold a magnificent archangel of golden light.

Downy soft wings reached to the ceiling.

Gossamer robe twinkled like a million stars.

Hair like gleaming sunlight.

Eyes of sapphire.

And a smile that reached in to warm my heart and surround it with total love.

All this was taken in as an instantaneous subliminal vision before the Visitor transformed into a traditionally clothed modern-day man with a gently pulsating golden aura about him.

My mind heard the unspoken words.

"I come from the Most High. I come with a message." And with that transmitted, he approached the love seat across from me and slowly lowered himself upon it.

Subconsciously, my own reaction surprised me. I'd accepted the Presence as though he were an old friend who'd stopped by to say "Hi" and this had amused me somewhat.

"What message brings you here?" I asked after feeling a new heaviness fill the room.

"A great concern."

"Concern?"

"A great concern that sets heavy on our hearts."

"*Our* hearts?"

His graceful arms outstretched. "Yes, ours. God and all the Powers of Light. The knowledge of our concern must be made known."

His words, though most sincere, reminded me of another who once claimed I needed to serve as a messenger and that hadn't been as easy to carry through as it sounded.

I softly responded. "These are difficult times for messages," I tried to explain. "Too many out there giving them out, too many claims, too many ego trips."

My guest's head bowed before his eyes again met my own. "Will you hear our concern?"

"Of course," I whispered. "I hadn't meant to deter you nor put you off, I only wanted you to know this world is overflowing with spiritual garbage that nobody seems to smell."

The man's aura flared. "Yes," came the sad reply, "we know. This is part of our concern. May I begin?"

He required no verbal response from me as I resettled myself back into my reading chair.

The firelight danced over the walls yet couldn't soften the deep concern on his countenance.

The pitch in the logs snapped and crackled as the archangel sitting before me slowly began a tale of human woe.

"I come with a grave message. I come not to reveal esoteric secrets nor psychic ways to power. No metaphysics. No revelations. . .except a sure and solid prophecy. This last I will speak of only after I have detailed Our concern."

He paused.

I remained silent. Attentive.

He began again with a question. "If I were to ask you what was the greatest cause of negativity in the world, what would your answer be?"

"Ego," I immediately responded.

His brow rose. "Why?"

"Because I've seen too much of it. I see it causing all manner of destruction. It ruins people's lives, it craves power of all types. The 'I' of the Self becomes an insatiable monster that destroys everything and everyone in its path. Ego is self-absorption. Ego kills."

"Yes, Ego." He sighed ever so softly. "We see the ego as a great contributor to the currently lowered collective consciousness — spiritual state — of humankind. It is smothering sensitivity and suffocating basic principles. Indeed, the rise in Self-importance has gravely impaired the opportunity to grow into the Spiritual Light. We watch as love of Self rises in priority on earth while love of others diminishes. Ego breeds apathy and denial. This we are greatly concerned over."

"Is this your message? To love others before Self?"

"I've not even begun," was his whispered reply.

And the sorrow I felt from those four words speared my heart as I braced for whatever was yet to come from this beautiful archangel's pristine soul.

"Clarification is needed between two transposed terms related to problems and their ensuing negativity caused by the ego. One psychological malfunction of the ego is what you term an inferiority complex, the other is self-absorption. These two are frequently misidentified and misdiagnosed as one for the other.

"An inferiority complex *lacks* ego. Self-absorption is *consumed* with ego."

I'd had personal experience with this in my life and I'd learned too late to recognize the difference between the two. I saw first hand how easily a self-absorbed individual claimed to have an inferiority complex when all the while *control* of others and a constant emphasis on Self was foremost in the mind. Control. Manipulation. Self. And when the control began to slip away, any means at all was utilized in an effort to regain it. Lies. Violence. Psychological and emotional manipulation. Jealousy.

My thoughts ended in a barely audible moan. "People die of self-consumption."

"Yes. Yes, they do. And they kill many other relationships along the way." His response startled me out of my musings.

"I'm sorry, I guess I was lost in thought. I hadn't meant to wander off."

"You were, shall we say, processing. Merely processing." He paused before continuing. "The message I came to give is not a lesson in the Spiritual Way but rather *how* humankind is *acting* now. The behavior of each individual is either generally negative or positive. This general behavior constitutes the overall *collective* consciousness of a civilization." He paused.

I could see where he was going. "Your message is like the President's State of the Union Address, isn't it. It's to make a kind of declaration — a State of the Human Soul Address."

The corner of his mouth tipped up in a slight smile. "People need to see that state — how they're behaving and what the consequences will be if they continue on their current course."

"Consequences? Is that the prophecy you mentioned before?"

"It is."

I had the distinct feeling that this prophecy was going to turn out to be more like the writing-on-the-wall instead of anything new. My gaze rested upon the flames in the opened woodstove. My entire being experienced a dense wave of empathy wash through it. I turned my attention back to the Visitor.

"I think it's too late for your message, your prophecy."

"What is time?" the gentle voice asked. "Time is not dates, not *real* time. Real Time resides within the Mind of God. Hours, dates mean nothing in the Reality of All That Is."

"Time. Dates," I repeated. "You'd never know that in respect to the upcoming millennium."

He nearly chuckled. "They don't recall the many millenniums that have already passed into history. They don't. . .remember. You see, it's the ego factor that makes this millennium significant to them. This is the one *they* experience, therefore it must carry some powerful or momentous event along with it."

I was hesitant. "You know of the various expectations and predictions for that date?"

"People," he said nodding, "require more time to turn things around. The 2001 date will not be enough. God is generous."

"It's all apocalyptic, you know."

"Fear is most prevalent in the minds of the ignorant," was his only comment.

The snapping fire spoke for a while and we listened to it as though it were the ticking of Earth's clock.

Reflections danced upon the patchwork quilt on the love seat and brought the bright colors to life as I myself reflected on what the archangel had said. Perhaps my own recent lesson in having faith was what ignited the new thought. I had to have my stirring optimism verified one way or the other.

"Though I know your message has just begun and it will likely cover much negative human behavior, I'm of the opinion you're offering. . .hope."

"Hope?"

"Yes, I was once lead to believe that there was hope for humankind and this beautiful planet, but then another dashed those hopes."

"Hopes can only be dashed if one gives up. God is all merciful. I believe you were shown an outcome that resulted from a collective fatalism. People need to understand the message — negative behavior breeds destruction. They have time to alter that outcome. That is the message."

My eyes brightened. "Then there *is* hope!"

"Let us continue," came the grave tone that brought me back to the present state of the human General Consciousness.

"We may as well begin with this apocalyptic aspect that is so prevalent in what is termed New Age philosophy and also with those who are upon a narrow, bible-minded path. Both are obsessive. They are too energetically focused on punishment, negativity. The idea of Dark Forces rule their lives. The New Agers focus on negative vibrations and the bible-toters dwell so much on the issue and persona of Satan it would appear he is more fascinating than God.

"So here we see a basic preoccupation with negativity. Dark Forces. Negative Vibrations. Devils and Demons. With this comes, hand-in-hand, a misguided perception of power that is evidenced by the speaking-in-tongues claim. This is pure ego of Self seeking control of others through a pseudo-spiritual venue. Whether a new-ager claims to channel or a born-again claims to lead a group by way of a so-called Divine

Voice makes no difference. It's the power, the control, they're craving."

I responded immediately. "I think this is becoming more obvious as time passes. Knowledge, secret or otherwise, isn't power — wisdom is. Yet true and pure messages, personal insights, are given to people."

"This is so, however, here we're addressing the specific prevalence of those negatively-generated communications based on and within the ego itself, those that are not true transmissions."

"You're referring to what I call the spiritual garbage."

Again the corner of his mouth tipped up. "We tend to see it as spiritual arrogance. Yet so few humans base their beliefs on the simplicity and unencumbered fact of God's pure love. It would appear that fear of the devil keeps people in check more than the desire of wanting God's love. That is a great concern for us."

I frowned. "That's really a sad way to put it but I see it as Ego and Fear ruling lives instead of Love and Faith. Somewhere along the line Love, even the very word, has lost its power. It's almost become a cliché or an overused or heard tune. Do you know what I'm trying to say?"

He nodded as I continued.

"Love seems to be old hat. To me it appears that people think it's so much more interesting to seek out mystery ways, esoteric secrets, little-known paths to one power or another, yet all along, pure goodness and right living is all that's needed to get back to God."

"Yes, it is so. The Way has become too simple. It's become. . .uninteresting — even boring."

The archangel's voice matched his countenance — grief-filled. Though I'd frequently felt anger over this same issue, the sorrow I now felt issuing forth from him speared through my soul.

"They've time to change, right?" I tried.

Silence.

I leaned forward in an attempt to catch his eye. "They've time to change, right?"

He acknowledged my insistent question. . .our eyes locked. "Time to change, alter their behavior. Yes."

The response lacked the convincing tone I'd sought. "There's a 'but' in there somewhere. You hold doubts."

"Doubt is too negative. We hold concern, reservations," he said.

"But isn't that why you've come? People can change, they can tone down their daily negativity if they understand that, by doing so, they'll raise the collective consciousness of the human race. They can center on love more often, not let fears dominate their lives, get back to spiritual simplicity instead of looking here and there for mystery ways." I brightened. "Right?"

"Perhaps."

"But there's more, isn't there."

"Yes. More."

I rested back in the chair once again while thinking that the state of the human soul wasn't in a very healthy condition.

Then, another question was posed to me. "Do you know how many times we hear people blaming God for something in their lives?"

I shook my head. "I imagine it's a lot. People also think to thank God too."

This effort to even out the score didn't help matters at all.

The archangel sighed. "People don't understand God so they blame Him for the bad things He didn't do or didn't *allow* to happen and they thank Him for the good things people should be accrediting to their *own* efforts.

"A football player gets down and crosses himself after a touchdown is made. He's thanking God for the score. God had no part in that. The player did it through his own efforts. That's misplaced credit. That's evidence that the player believed God had a hand in his good fortune.

"And a mother who blames God for a child's illness or death is misinterpreting blame for reality. God does not randomly pass out illness tickets or death sentences. God merely *watches*. He watches and observes what is done with what one has to work with. He watches for inner strength and acceptance, resourcefulness, and reason. To thank God for a winning lottery ticket is ludicrous.

"People need to understand the idea of Free Will and the choices that it presents. Positive and negative events and situations are continually presented in life as a *natural* unfolding. How one utilizes the choices out of probable responses and alternatives is decidedly up to them, not a gift or a curse from God."

Again I attempted to soften the harshness of the words I'd heard. "We have blessings, though. We count blessings."

"A blessing is an individualized perspective, is it not?"

I ran that new idea through my mind.

He continued before I could comment. "You count a sunny day or a particularly enjoyable nature sighting or experience as a blessing whereas your neighbor may not be so moved by such."

"Still. . .it's a blessing to me, they're among the ones I count. My neighbor may count a successful soufflé as a blessing but she still has a blessing to count."

The man smiled. Actually smiled.

I grinned back. "Right?"

"Right. Yet so many are blind to these blessings — these simple causes for great joy in one's daily life. Few people realize the beautiful effect a smile can have on a stranger who is having a bad day. A kind word. A prayer for another. A positive thought directed toward a perceived enemy. These are blessings *given* — those that one can bestow on another. All blessings don't have to be *received* to be counted as such and appreciated."

Again he made me think. He was right. People weren't really aware of the little acts of goodness they performed throughout their day. They needed to realize the goodness in themselves and then recognize it as manifested spiritual acts instead of focusing so much on the negatives in their lives. And I wanted to find a way to get that helpful concept across to folks. I made a mental note to figure out later how I could accomplish this.

A log loudly popped and awakened my attention back to the night Visitor. When our eyes met I felt I'd been an errant listener to have wandered off as I had. . .except he was stifling a grin.

"What?" I instinctively said.

He pretended innocence. "Did I say anything?"

"Well," I hesitated, "you may have while I was wandering off in my head. I'm sorry."

His grin widened. "You'll find your way."

"Way to where?"

"Let's continue." He'd cut me off and I let it go. Somewhere along the line I'd lost the thread of our dialogue and it bothered me. To cover my discomfort I got up to check the fire. It didn't need restoking and I resettled myself.

"Do you know who I am?" he questioned.

It seemed he asked a lot of questions; at least he appeared to begin each new subject matter in this manner.

I responded. "You chose to present yourself as an archangel when you first appeared. I understood that to be your intent to indicate who you are."

"And my name?"

"That came as an automatic knowing, but aren't names irrelevant?" Indeed, knowing who he was upon his initial manifestation was a spiritual shock that jarred my very soul, yet there also was an inherent acceptance that carried its own message. LISTEN TO HIM! THIS IS IMPORTANT FOR THE WORLD!

"Yes," he responded, "irrelevant. As irrelevant as your own."

The side comment made my skin tingle. "I don't believe I'm the subject of this visitation. We were discussing the current state of human souls."

He smiled. "And beliefs. The superfluous and the real of them."

My palms upturned. "There are more variations to the Spiritual Truths than flowers growing in a wild mountain meadow."

"We see this."

Well, I thought, what a dumb thing I'd said, of course they knew that. I blushed.

He kindly ignored my embarrassment by getting right into the issue. "Human spiritual beliefs are mostly nonexistent. What has become a disappointing development to us is the fact that the basic and pure *spiritual* truths have been smothered by embellishments of the human-created *religions*. The proof of this directly rests upon the endless rituals performed by the various religions. God asks for no rituals, special prayers, special feast days, or ceremonial objects. Neither is God sexist nor a racist, therefore would never generate a rule that disqualified a woman from becoming a priest (if He required such an individual, which He does not). You see where I'm going? Where do all these superfluous aspects come from?"

I did. It had been clear to me for a long while that, when delving into the fundamental facets of the different religions and how they historically came into being, most all were based on a male-dominated perspective. I wasn't interested right now in getting heavily involved in this embroiling issue so I opted to simply nod my head in response to his question.

He glanced toward the dancing flames in the woodstove. Then, meeting my eyes, he continued.

"These religions are of great concern to us because they are so full of extra dogma, man-made rules and unnecessary demands that they've resulted in a cluttering of the basic truths and simple way to God.

"These religions have literally grown into a separate power, their own power, so much so, they have become a type of god in and of themselves. Some, to the point of being idolatrous!"

I am the Lord thy God. Thou shalt not have strange gods before Me. The words of the First

Commandment reverberated through my mind like the booming voice of God Himself.

I attempted an explanation. "People think they need ritual and ceremony. They believe grand vestments and accouterments enhance their beliefs."

The Visitor raised his voice for the first time. "Enhancements? *God* needs no *enhancements!*"

I was at a loss for a way to respond. Of course I knew God needed no enhancing and I couldn't come up with any viable reason for why folks needed the extra fluff around their beliefs. The silence between us was embarrassing me. It was weighted.

The Visitor's words made the room's atmosphere heavier. "What sort of so-called enhancement was the Inquisition? How did that serve to enhance the Catholic Church?"

I grimaced with his reminder of such a spiritually arrogant and inhumanely cruel historical period.

Suddenly the archangel's voice emitted from somewhere other than the love seat across from me. He'd moved without my notice and was standing in front of the stone wall beside the woodstove. He began to pace before the firelight that could not reflect over him; his own beingness was a light of itself. Firelight flickered over the stones behind him, yet not upon his form.

He spoke. "Do you see proof of any false dogma through the former existence of the Inquisition?"

The only thing that came to mind was the religious statement that had been drilled into me as a child, a dogmatic belief I'd long shed.

"The specific man-made idea that the Pope always speaks and acts for God. . .that the Pope is infallible. I don't believe God could've devised something as cruel and evil as the Inquisition. Over time I've come to see that, throughout history, God chooses many to speak for Him but none are infallible. Only God Himself is infallible. Claiming to be an infallible voice for God is a grab for religious power. . .control. It's the height of spiritual arrogance."

The angel lowered his gaze to the snapping fire. His tone reflected a heavy heart. "This is evidenced by others too, not just the Pope. Ego drives many to claim the Lord's voice and," he paused, "and God's message — the Word — becomes hopelessly bastardized.

"We are concerned to hear of a current belief in human godheads — people believing they are as gods and goddesses unto themselves." His eyes locked on mine. "Is that not having other gods before the Lord? Is that not idolatry in its most arrogant and egotistical form?"

I had to agree. "It's making the Self equal to God. Just because we possess a fragment of God's beautiful beingness within our soul doesn't come close to having the totality of Him." I sighed. "We are God's children. We are *of* God. That doesn't make us gods too." My voice lowered to a whisper. "God must be very sad over this. This must cause Him much heart pain."

"We are all sad over this, yet idolatry appears to be running rampant in the world. People are even making the Blessed Mother Mary into the subject of their worship. . .to the point of praying to her instead of their Lord God, to the point of making her their center of religious focus instead of God Himself. She has even been accredited with more power than God." The archangel shook his head. "Little tiny gods and goddesses feeding their egos by self-aggrandizement, pretenders claiming to speak for false gods and goddesses while perpetrating idolatry."

I felt so bad I could find no words with which to soothe his grief. Neither of us spoke for a moment or two as we listened to the crackling fire try to cheer up the room's sorrowful atmosphere.

Finally I came up with something to say. "I feel a growing desperation whenever I'm out among people. I don't leave the cabin much, but when I do, I'm surrounded by a strong aura of hopelessness, a sort of general apathy. People seem to be in some sort of frantic state; traffic is hectic and the overall vibrations of those I pass are spiking and erratic. I feel a rushing all around me, almost a sense of panic in folks. It's extremely unsettling for me and I'm always relieved to get back home to the calm of the cabin again. There's no denying that people are restless. They're searching for something they can't name — just *something* to give greater meaning to their lives, their future holds no security, no hope."

The archangel's brow rose in question. "*God* holds no hope for them? They are not secure in His *love* for them?"

"For many I'm sure that's true, but I'm referring to the general masses."

"So am I. I too am referring to the masses here and we see them making a god of God's messengers and even of their religions. Their religions — their individualized spiritual ideologies — have become as gods in themselves and these they make wars over, these they kill for."

"The Crusades?"

"They never stopped. Spiritual wars continue to this very hour and they're an abomination to God." He sighed. "Even Jesus the messenger is currently perceived as a god and adored above the Lord God."

"The Word gets lost in the physical beingness of the messenger," I interjected. "I know that's wrong but it appears to be the nature of humans to need a touchable representative of the given Word."

"That's because they've lost their *touch* with God," he said sorrowfully.

"Perhaps." My one word response was a feeble one and we both knew it. We both knew that people had lost the beautiful feel of God's presence within them.

My Visitor's eyes locked on mine. "Why are you placing yourself in the position of their advocate? There is no defense for their actions."

"I'm not sure why I'm doing that. I've recognized these negatives that have been eating away at spirituality and I've grieved over them and prayed over them. I've even shed a tear or two because of them. Maybe I'm trying to soften the harshness of it all. I believe people can turn it around."

"So do we. So do we or I wouldn't be standing before you now. Their behavior and what needs to be changed must be pointed out and brought to their attention. They need to understand that it's *because* of their penchant to make gods of the messengers that all these current religious fragments exist. The God of Abraham is the same God of Jesus. The God of Mohammed is the same God of Martin Luther. The God of Joseph Smith is the same God of the Fundamentalists. Yet it is the *human* aspect that has added to and subtracted from God's pure and simple spiritual Truths that were given as the Word in the beginning. If people, with their inflated egos, didn't think the Word needed enhancing according to their multitudinous human conditions, personal perspectives, or societal mores, there would've been one world religion — God's pure Word."

I nodded. "I'm not playing advocate again, but it's all in the interpretation, isn't it. People feel the need to pick things apart and analyze everything. The philosopher will interpret differently from what the shoemaker concludes, the scientist will see it differently from the rabbi. Just one simple statement of Truth can end up with a thousand faces." I smiled. "Sort of like all the many religions being cupcakes made from the same basic recipe. . .just decorated differently."

The archangel grinned too. "Yes, then fighting over whose is right because the decorations conceal the basic common ingredients of the original Word."

I sighed. "It's so easy to see how it all got started. All because people connected a separate God to each messenger instead of realizing that each messenger speaks for the one God."

The man's grin widened. "Someday, if humans don't understand this, there will be The God of Summer Rain!"

I was aghast. "No."

"I'm attempting humor here."

"That was not funny to me! That was not one bit amusing. I'm trying very hard to keep my presence, my beingness, out of the public eye because that's the only way it should be for a messenger. Remember? No razzle-dazzle. No ego coming in? No walking on water?" I began getting animated. "My God, these people are even equating the beings from other planets to gods!" There were many nights I stared out into the woods wondering if humankind could ever find its way back from such a sorry state of affairs through their need to complicate the Word's simplicity.

I hadn't realized how hard I'd been thinking on this for the angel had moved over to the window when I next gave Him attention. He made no comment regarding my personal introspection, instead he expanded on the subject.

"Idolatry, false gods, doesn't only refer to the misplaced adoration of God's messengers. We see people making gods of money and power, their status and position. Beauty. Drugs. Fame. Control and manipulation. The Self. All these constitute a form of Idolatry when prioritized above God and the Word of God."

Things. Stuff. Ego. I wondered why God wasn't the most important goal in life. Why were people so obsessed with the Self to the point of causing their spirituality and its Way to be secondary? "Ego appears to be the root of many evils," I said.

"So it seems. Ego and all that feeds its voracious appetite."

And with the moment of silence that trailed his last statement, I took the opportunity to tend to the fire. It needed no tending and that fact made me frown as I settled back into my chair.

"We hear a great cry rise — a cry that curses God," announced the archangel.

Thou shalt not take the name of the Lord thy God in vain, I thought while I listened.

"This business of placing blame on God, we need to expand on that. Cursing God means blaming God. When someone curses another they are taking this other individual's name in vain, they are angry. Anger directed to another equates to blame of some other deeply-felt negative emotion connected to the individual. These kinds of dark thoughts and energies should never be associated with the all-loving and compassionate Lord God."

"You're talking about the Second Commandment."

"Yes."

"People think that means no swearing."

"People are wrong then. Swearing is a superficial response. It holds no depth of meaning. Blame is a deep-seated real attitude. God knows the difference; people should too. Taking God's name in vain means to seriously and *intentionally* place blame on Him as though He were personally singling out people and choosing who will experience great grief or hard times."

I shook my head. "That's so ridiculous it sounds positively silly, yet I also believe people instinctively know this."

"Of course some do, however, there are far too many who do not. These ones wholeheartedly believe that God orchestrates their entire life and these people are the ones who fear making their own decisions based on the beautiful Free Will God gave them. To them, Free Will means following the life course *God* set for them instead of the course they are supposed to choose for themselves. Therefore, every bad event that happens to them is believed to have been a personal directive from God, hence the ensuing blame.

"Conversely," he said, "we see these same people thanking God for the good events in their lives — good outcomes they themselves have brought to fruition. These people cannot seem to understand that they are completely on their own for the duration of their time in the physical. They forget that God's great gift to them is the Free Will and, without it, there would be no reason to exist."

I hadn't thought of life in that context before, yet the concept was so simple: Free Will gave our lives meaning. Indeed, why live in the physical if every footfall was orchestrated by God, or anyone else? Why, we'd be nothing more than puppets if that were the case. And God doesn't want us doing right because we're *forced* to; He wants us doing right because we *choose* to. It was the *choosing* — the basic knowledge of having choices — that freed us to set our own course back to God. And it was this freely-chosen course that determined what events and situations it would contain and how it would ultimately conclude.

The archangel caught my attention then. "You see how illogical it is for people to blame God. They are needing a scapegoat and placing false blame."

I nodded. "It stands to reason, doesn't it? I mean, when one doesn't recognize that all they do in life is his or her own responsibility then, whenever things go awry, they don't take personal responsibility for the outcome. Also I believe guilt plays a factor too. I think a lot of people don't want to carry guilt so they place blame on the shoulders of another. . .then try to convince themselves that this is true."

The man's voice was soft as baby's breath. "You've been made the scapegoat now and again."

My gaze shifted over to the dancing flames. "I'm healing right now. I don't want to talk about me."

He didn't quite agree. "I think it's important to see how these negative behaviors affect everyone's life, even your own. It brings home the prevalence of what our message is and how widespread it has become. Too frequently people deny these negativities that touch their lives. Too often they choose to be blind to what is happening around them while their rosy-colored glasses make false views of their perceptions."

I looked square up at him. "While this is true, I'm not one of those wearing any colored glasses, so why the need to get personal with all this?"

"The *need* is for the purpose of clarifying a depiction of such prevalence — that much of people's negative behavior touches even *your* life."

I frowned at that. "Just what are you getting at? People don't *know* all that's touched my life and won't know unless someone tells them."

His countenance remained unchanged. The brilliance of his blue eyes remained locked on mine. "Will our message end here? With you? Will it stay locked within this cabin room? Never to reach those who will change their ways and raise the Collective Consciousness?"

His intent was as clear and sharp as a hawk's cry.

And he'd felt my new heaviness. "You think we're insensitive to all you've recently been through? I think not. Though you're doing well at healing, do you believe your purpose takes a vacation?"

"Do *you* believe I believe that?" I interrupted.

"We were talking of what *you* believe," he immediately responded back. "We know you don't believe that because you know that's not how it works. Though you thought you'd take a break from writing, does that mean the Word won't be given until you are ready to share it? We all know that's not so. Your commitment is too strong, far too ingrained. Your daily plane of existence naturally overrides the negatives of this physical life you have to trudge through for a while. Yes, you need to heal on several lower levels, yet your predominate level needs no healing. It is as strong and vibrantly vital as ever." He cocked his head. "Is it not?"

I didn't respond. My head was full of cascading thoughts that his words had poured forth.

Finally, I managed to display a slight smile that acknowledged the truth to his words.

His eyes sparkled like stars on a cold winter night when he grinned back at me.

"This is a heavy place," I commented. "It's the 'I' planet. The Planet of Ego. Of Self. One of the most psychologically dense and difficult places to work on."

"Yes."

My eyes scanned the little cozy room. "This is my sanctuary, this is the only place I feel at home."

He knew what I meant by that. "Home. We know you miss it," he comforted while glancing around and deeply inhaling the scent of cedar I'd been burning. "Like the calm of a quiet church when you're the only visitor."

I nodded. "And the forest out there, the woods. . .those woods are so fresh and pure. They send out their own aura of serenity."

"And," he said, "the wildlife too?"

"Sometimes. Being out here, having the opportunity to observe so many animals has opened my eyes. They too experience jealousy and violent behavior among themselves. I've watched several families of deer come to feed just beyond those windows and, although I was thrilled to observe their mating ritual – how they flirted with each other – I've also seen dominate bucks come up the rise to feed and all the others giving him plenty of room while the does will strike out and hit the backs of their small yearlings with a foreleg in order to get a better position at the fresh grain for themselves. I've watched the bucks challenge each other, yet I've also anxiously watched with held breath as Sally walks out there at night to open a fresh grain bag while a large buck stands not four feet away, closely observing her every move.

"I saw a red-tailed hawk swoop down right in front of me to grab up a rabbit and fly off with it. I've watched birds fight one another over one sunflower seed when the feeder was brimming. Squirrels chasing each other away from their full feeder. A raccoon eating out of my friend's hand and, one night I saw the raccoon pair nuzzling each other. A bird sitting on my shoulder brought such joy, a flock of them feeding around my feet make me giggle. I saw a coyote pounce on a hiding mouse, then play with it for a long time. And I've watched two pair of great horned owls perch on a winter-bare aspen to eye my tiny Yorkie, Pinecone. . .she's only two pounds, you know. She'd make nothing more than a snack for those owls." My shoulders slumped. "The wildlife gives me wondrous joys and deep sorrows while observing their hard life lived for daily survival. They too have a wide range of behavior. . .just like people."

"However," he quickly added, "animals don't have reason."

I tilted my head. "Don't they? I've observed the cleverness of too many animals to agree with your statement. I have another little Yorkie named Rosebud. She believes she's the official Toy Master of all the dog toys. Her favorite house game is fetch and, if Sally or I throw her ball into a particularly difficult place, she's so one-minded that she'll spend all day trying to figure out a route to that ball. Rosie is very intelligent and she always ends up with that ball in her mouth. As I watch her, I can almost hear her mind analyzing different plans as she looks from a chair to the hidden ball, then looks to the table or counter and back to the ball; pacing and testing all the while until she figures it out. I've watched the wildlife too. They can be exceedingly clever."

My Visitor smiled, "I should've been more definitive with you. Animals have no knowledge of God."

I grinned. "Now that I would accept because it's the knowledge of God and His Word that differentiates the right and the wrong behavior of humans."

"We're back on track," he advised, "and people need to realize how prevalent their negative behavior is in the world. They need to realize how much of it touches their own lives and. . ."

"Even my life," I finished. "I thought we'd gotten off that subject."

"*You* left it. I never did."

I sighed. This was one focused archangel.

He ignored my unspoken thought and jumped right into his next subject. "A while ago we were speaking of beliefs, both religious and spiritual. Now I need to emphasize how important it is to *live* those beliefs on an *hourly* basis instead of being of a mind to make these beliefs confined to a special day."

Thou shalt keep holy the Sabbath ran through my mind. I voiced the thought.

"Yes," he affirmed. "We will have discussed all ten by the time my message has concluded. These ten statements are the only laws God expects people to live by. So simple, isn't it? Yet even these have been misinterpreted and expanded upon by humans throughout history.

"The Third Commandment has been taken to mean: Make one holy day out of the week and honor God on that day. This was *never* the original intent. Keep *holy* the *Sabbath*. Holy refers to the *practice* and Sabbath refers to *spirituality*. The original intent was this: Keep Spirituality in your life! Keep it in your *heart* throughout your *daily* life! It's not even logical that God would want only one day out of seven to be a spiritual one. It's not logical that God would want people's attention to center on the spiritual on just a specified day. He wants people to *live* His laws on an *hourly* basis. God being first and foremost. . .*always*.

"A secondary aspect of this," he expanded, "is what we hear being called the Holiday Spirit, the Christmas Spirit. What are those supposed to mean?"

"Those phrases have recently bothered me too," I said. "Although the Holiday and Christmas Spirit is supposed to mean goodwill and spiritual joy, I began to be somewhat irritated every time I heard those words spoken. I was irritated that there was a specialness – a specific *season* –

for the practice of goodwill and spiritual joy instead of *living* them year-round." I sighed. "I don't know what they're supposed to mean because what they mean to the masses is stupid to me. The Holiday Spirit shouldn't be any different than how people act or feel every day. God takes no holiday from people's lives. He's there every hour for them. And what makes a *Christmas* Spirit anyway?"

The Archangel raised his hands in a halting gesture. "Slow down. We seem to be of the same mind over these issues. Let's talk about this Christmas idea. It falls under the subject at hand. Tell me what event Christmas marks?"

"People believe it marks the birth of Christ. Jesus Christ. Christ. . .the Lord."

His hand was on his chin in a contemplative attitude. "Christ. Christ. . .the Lord."

"I know," I commented, "there's only one Lord. . .Lord God. They made a god of God's Male Aspect, what is termed: His Son, called Jesus."

"We need to take this thread and angle off onto this issue. I was going to discuss the Triad of God's beingness — the Trinity — later in our discourse but it presented now so we'll cover it at this time.

"There is a Triad to God's beingness. There is the Pure Essence of God which *we* know as the Mother/Father persona which, unfortunately, humans believe as only being a father image. Then there is God's Male Aspect which could be called Son. And there is His Female Aspect which has been erroneously called Holy Spirit. His Female Aspect is called Daughter or Shekhinah. Both the aspects of Daughter and Son have entered the world countless times as spiritual messengers. And, sadly, it was a rarity when the people didn't make a god or a new religion out of them. The Son was known by many names, so was the Daughter, Shekhinah, who has at long last come to be recognized as God's Spirit at work in the world."

"Religions have a male focus," I informed. "People will have a difficult time perceiving and accepting the Holy Spirit as God's Female Aspect."

"Why? God is balanced. If He has a uniquely defined Male Aspect will He not be unbalanced if He has no Female Aspect? How difficult can that be to understand?"

I shrugged. "Well you know it's true and I know it's true but. . ."

"Mary!"

"What!"

"It's *time!*"

"It was time *ages* ago but. . ."

"Mary!"

"What!"

"Why is there always a *but*?"

"Because there usually is. This time there is. I know Jesus tried to clarify this yet the people back then, as now, were of a completely male-dominated society. They couldn't bring themselves to accept a Female Aspect of God being equal to a Male Aspect of God. Females were perceived as a lesser being and therefore held lower status. No matter how hard and no matter how many different ways Jesus tried to explain this, the concept was one of those spiritual truths that was not accepted. So then they came up with that Holy Ghost idea as some sort of compromise. That was. . ."

"Mary?" came the soft voice.

"What."

"Why are you telling *me* all this?"

"Because I got riled up. I get very impassioned over this and it carried me away. How silly of me to go on and on about something you already know." I sheepishly grinned. "I'm sorry."

"Sorry? What for? It's that kind of enthusiasm for the truth that makes God smile."

"Enthusiasm? I would say it was more like disgust over the ongoing belief in spiritual fallacies."

"Mary?"

"What."

"That's why I've come. That's why I'm here by your fireside. It's time to reveal certain truths, straighten out misinterpretations, open up the eyes."

"Many eyes here are purposely closed. They are in denial. They pick and choose that which they want to accept, hear and see."

The archangel's eyes glistened. "So we give them another choice!"

His answer wasn't as encouraging as he anticipated it to be for me yet. I didn't bother to debate his hopeful premise. Instead, I got up to restock the woodstove. Picking up a piece of aspen, I frowned and dropped it back on top of the pile. I looked to the man who had moved beside me. "The fire — it. . .never mind," I muttered, returning to the chair. Cheyenne, my Keeshond, had settled herself beneath it while I'd been at the woodstove. She must've been comfortable with our visitor as her eyes were already drooping with the drowsiness that the woodstove warmth always brought to her. When I sat down, Punkin Pie, my other Yorkie pup, jumped into my lap and snuggled down for a cozy nap. Pinecone followed suit and my attention turned to stroking their soft little heads. Several moments of gentle silence passed before my gaze went to the votive candle burning on the table, then crossed to settle on my visitor. "The light of the flame can only be perceived and appreciated when it's dark," I said. "The flame, the flame itself can always be seen, but the *light* that flame sheds — the actual illumination — can only be seen and appreciated when it's dark."

He moved to the love seat and sat down, listening to my words. "So too is the illumination of the flames of truth you bring."

I glanced over at the flickering fire flames then back to the man's calm face. "How dark must it get before they see?"

"Many see with their soul, their heart. It's these we're counting on."

"And by your count. . .it's enough?"

"It's enough for me to be here. It's enough to make the sharing of our message a worthwhile effort."

Silence.

"You don't think so too?" he asked.

I bowed my head. Rubbing the little furry necks of the sweet ones in my lap made me want to get lost in their innocence.

The archangel leaned forward to peer up at me. "You don't much like working here, do you."

I remained unresponsive.

He rested back and gazed out the window, returning his attention only when I finally whispered a reply.

"It's so dense. So backward. . .so physically base here."

He kindly made no reference to the mistiness covering my eyes, yet his voice was sympathetic. "Yes. The density of the ego is always darkened by its very nature, which contains the lowest negative qualities. This is why so much violence prevails here. This is why it's a sexually oriented environment and so many forms of control — manipulative behavior — exist. It's not a spiritually fertile atmosphere to work within." He paused. "I'm sorry."

Our eyes met. "It *could* be a spiritually fertile environment if they'd only focus on God instead of all their plastic gods."

"Yes. . ."

"It's so hard in this day and age," I said. "They're all looking for and awaiting the fantastic. They're grasping at reflections on office building windows thinking they see Mary or Jesus or whoever. They're seeing crosses in cloud formations and reading dialogues with God. Paintings that cry or bleed." My head slowly went from side to side. "How does the simplicity of the Word stand a chance when these people are in such high expectation for the most fantastic and seemingly ultimate manifestation? Their own expectation for the spectacular blinds them to the simple truths that are always before them. They ignore that which doesn't dazzle."

He made no reply as I continued to voice my thoughts.

"For the life of me I cannot understand why God's love isn't enough dazzle to satisfy them. I can't imagine that *seeing* has become more desirable than *feeling*. I keep telling them to go within to find peace and God but few seem to grasp the magnitude of what that means. How is it that that's become some complex thing? It's too simple, that's the reason. They want more. They want the complex patterns, a mesmerizing and hypnotic kaleidoscopic vision that amazes the mind and dazzles the eye. They want physical because they're physical." I looked down at the sleeping puppies again. "It's not working. This place is too physical, they're like little kids whose eyes only widen at the sight of the Christmas tree lights instead of the *reason* for the tree. It's a touchy-feelie mind set. Nobody feels unless something can be touched with false awe through the fingertips. I can't offer glitter for them. I can't offer the spectacular for them to. . ."

"Nobody asked you to," he interrupted.

". . .for them to flock to and get hysterical over." I finished. "At this late date people have got to recognize the Truth and believe it by the beautiful warmth that the natural *Knowing* brings to them. That's the only way it was meant to happen with messengers and that's the way I've worked to adhere to. But. . ."

"But you feel defeated. You feel ineffective."

"Of course I do. Plain and Simple gets lost in *Spectacular*. Gentle whispers of Truth get silenced under false spiritual *roars*. The flame's illumination pales before the plastic *dazzle*. People are too entranced by the physical. They've traded in the very *Essence* of God for the love of spectacles. They want to *see* instead of feel. They want to touch this and touch that with their bare fingers instead of with their bare hearts. They want their Knowing to come from a physical experience, not from their soul."

I was so full of despair that my grief flowed forth. "And their prayers are not filled with words of adoration. They pray for Self! They pray for *their* wants instead of God's. Prayers to pass a test, for want of someone's love. Prayers to win a game or money. . .whatever. . .always asking, asking, asking."

"That issue was to be part of our message," he informed. "No more *special* days set aside for spiritual focus. No more ego-centered prayers. Less of the asking and much more of the honor given and expressions of acceptance and appreciation. More recognition of daily blessings instead of bemoaning the negatives. More acceptance of personal responsibility instead of making scapegoats of others and of God. Your shoulders are as slumped as ours. Your heart, as heavy."

"But you don't have to live here," I said.

"And you don't have to feel how prevalent it all is," he retorted.

I made a sad face. "I'm sorry. I only see a small percentage of the negative behavior. You see it all."

"Yes. We *feel* it all."

"So?"

"So?" he echoed.

"Well what am I to do? People crave the many gurus. They clamor for words from the Starborn ones. They hunger for and devour books or tapes by any channeler who comes along. These extravagances are thirsted for." A sharp heart pain speared through my chest. I winced. "They thirst not for the simple Word."

He expressed clear concern as I rubbed my chest. "Are you alright?"

"Yes. Yes, just a muscle stitch," I said while shifting my position a bit. "They don't thirst for the life-saving Spring Water, instead their tastes have changed; now they want flavored drinks — the more exotic the better. So. . .how do we get them back to water again?"

"The exotic will pale after a time and they'll come into their own realization that clear, fresh water quenches far better, is more satisfying in the end."

We sat in silence for awhile. I felt he was enjoying the tranquil atmosphere of the cabin. Pinecone and Punkin remained nestled on my lap, tiny paws twitched in their dreaming sleep. They were such a comfort to me. "These little, furry ones are so innocent," I whispered. "All they want to do is please me and they're so loving. They've got such cute personalities, each one different and unique."

"Almost like real children," the visitor added.

I nodded. "Except. . ."

"Except?"

"Nothing. Never mind."

"Except?" he pushed.

"Except these ones don't hurt a mother's heart."

"Yes. Their love is a constant emotion. It doesn't waver nor is it ever interfered with by the ego, which is a human affectation."

"Affliction. Defect," I corrected. "Ego is a human defect that harms all it touches, especially relationships."

"So then," he announced, "you've brought us to our next concern. Family relationships."

Thou shalt honor thy Father and thy Mother. We had progressed to the Fourth Commandment.

"Parental respect has been lost," he began. "This loss of respect and all its relative negatives can be traced to the malignant growth of the ego. It, more than any other element, has caused families to self-destruct.

"The 'I' wants physical pleasures, it wants to feel good — happy and even euphoric — so drugs are taken to achieve this. Drugs ruin the family unit. The father figure — the male ego — is reluctant to give up the old idea of being the head of the family, having the dominating power, and all forms of abuse ensue as an attempt to regain or maintain that position of control.

"Personal status, whether it be gauged by material possessions, type of employment, wealth, success, or popularity, is a family unit destroyer. The absorption with self, no matter what the form, denies the family the attentive physical, emotional, and interactive care required for the unit's natural function.

"We see children also being absorbed in the Self, bringing unreasonable expectations and demands of their parents. They decide they *know* better, want more of the material things *handed* to them, desire their *own* power, feel they *deserve* more than they have. These negatives grow out of an ever-expanding ego that ends up smothering love and respect. If even one member of a family unit is self-absorbed then the one destroys the whole. And the one will seek out other family members to blame if the one is not realizing self-satisfaction in every way. Hence there rises the physical, verbal, and emotional abuse, many times, all three."

The archangel's words brought a flood of memories to the forefront of my mind. Visions of different incidents that knotted my stomach and gripped my heart. Remembering un-characteristic behavior that was shocking to wit-ness, cruel statements made, hurtful stories spread. My eyes locked on my visitor's. "Ego kills all it touches," I said in deep sadness. "Ego even ends up killing its host. . .the Self."

The man gave a nod of agreement while lis-tening to my voiced thoughts on the matter.

"I've watched someone die of self-absorption and I've observed it everywhere throughout my life. I perceive it as a massive blanket darkly spreading over the world. That's why I made the statement earlier that this was the Ego Planet. Personal power, control, status, wealth, whatever, seem to be people's priorities. Ego causes racism, sexist attitudes, intolerance of others, violence, slander, jealousy, you name it. How can familial love and respect live and thrive when the chil-dren say 'me, me, me' and one of the parents demands dominance or is jealous of the other for whatever imagined reason? Familial love and respect can't exist in that kind of barren envi-ronment because when one doesn't *accept* the condition or quality of Self, one *can't* respect or love Self, hence respect or love for *others* is nonexistent."

He nodded. "We can also look to historical changes in societal perspectives that serve to generate negative responses based on ego. Even if the new alterations in perspective are positive ones, the ego can cause long-term havoc. A prime example of this was the forward step for gender equality. You know this as the Feminist Movement. And this was good," he reassured. "Only ego kept women on a perceived lower status throughout history. It was well past time to publicly recognize the intelligence, capabilities, and independent leadership qualities of the female gender. The Feminist Movement was not born out of a need or desire to claim gender superiority, but was manifested for the purpose of opening societal eyes and minds to the fact that females were *not* of a lesser, subservient or inferior class. The Movement gave balance. . .finally.

"So," he declared, "enter ego, the male ego. It now feels threatened. Its former strength, power, and dominance appears to be lessened, weakened and. . ."

"But it never really was," I interjected. "It was never lessened, it only had a female equal to *balance* it."

He smiled wide. "Yes! A wonderful balance!"

"Yet," I said, "men thought women sought superiority over them. They didn't understand what it was all about and failed to see the big picture. They feared losing their control and perceived higher status. It threatened them when wives began to realize they were individuals who were capable of getting good jobs and going back for a higher education, women realized they were capable of so much more than preparing dinners and changing diapers.

"I can see that the Movement would've been so much more universally beautiful if men hadn't taken it personally. They should've embraced it."

"Yes. And when they couldn't do that they rebelled. They rebelled because they saw their masculinity being threatened by the growing female presence within their worldly domain. This rebellion took many forms and it was then when spousal abuse increased, all because of being afraid to lose control, domination, and alleged superiority."

"Then," I said, continuing the thread, "women weren't taking that kind of abuse anymore. They realized they didn't have to because they weren't inferior to their mates. The women began seeking outside help and they left the relationships that were abusive. The incidents of divorce increased then and society ended up with single-parent families."

"All because of the male ego," he added. "Marriage has become something other than the partnership it was originally intended to be. And so we have a loss of love and respect between family members as being unique individuals comprising a beautiful whole. We see individualized expectations of the dominant ego making stringent demands on family members. Efforts at control and manipulation. A dangerous need to be recognized, attended to, and given priority. Families shatter because of these. They scatter to the wind. They become as strangers. Though we choose the family to be born in, destiny has a different path for each member."

"What are you saying? You seem to have jumped into another subject or have I missed something?"

"Perhaps I did fast forward with that last sentence. What needs to be understood is this: though a family be torn asunder, the life of each family member is not crippled, for every individual has her or his own unique destiny that is independent of a former family unit or the maintaining of those relationships."

"That sounds like a contradiction. How does one honor father and mother if that familial relationship loses importance?"

"That's not what I said. I never said or inferred that a father or mother loses importance. Your mother will always be your mother. Your father will always be your father. That relationship can never be changed." He smiled. "Well, it's a biological fact, isn't it. What we're saying here is this: families are an environment for learning and growth. Once one becomes an adult, he or she has a responsibility to follow her or his own unique destiny. . .independent of and separate from family members and familial philosophies."

"You're saying we need to accept and respect differing viewpoints of adult family members, no matter how much they differ from those once held as a familial unit when younger."

"Yes, as long as those different viewpoints are not negative ones. Acceptance of a sibling's different path, new philosophy, or life choice shows respect. This honors the other."

I grinned. "I once heard someone say that: 'just because your spirit chose to be born in a specific family doesn't necessarily mean you have to like them.' I thought about that statement and concluded that it was true. You may not particularly like someone in your family but you can still respect them and care about them."

"You've made a natural conclusion. Spirits enter into a family for varying personal reasons and they interact with family members until they reach adulthood and are then ready to follow the path they came to walk."

I grinned back. "Now you're talking about leaving the nest and striking out on one's own. That's just natural. I want to go back to the main issue of parental honor and respect. And, by the way, the reverse applies too — parents respecting their children. My issue is that respect doesn't inherently come hand-in-hand with parenting. What you said about parents being a biological fact, that's what I want to comment on. Respect doesn't automatically come with a title. The title of parent doesn't automatically mean one should be respected just because he or she became a mother or father due to a biological event. Respect is *earned*. One earns respect by honorable behavior. I hardly think Pope Gregory IX was respected much after he instigated the Inquisition that tortured and killed those who disagreed with the Church's teachings. Title means nothing if one's *behavior* isn't worthy and deserving enough to earn respect from others. Parents can't respect children who behave badly and, likewise, children can't be expected to respect parents who behave badly. If a man and a woman bring a child into the world, they as parents have the responsibility of setting good examples for them."

"This is true because this Commandment is directly associated with *authority* and encompasses all forms of it. The respect for authoritative figures is what the Fourth Commandment addresses. This would refer to law enforcement officers, teachers, parents, etc."

"But only if *they* exhibit proper behavior."

"Of course. This is what we've been talking about, is it not? However, overall respect for authority has become a deep concern to us because, on a global scale, we see it waning at an accelerated pace. It's waning because of the ego."

"Is it waning because authority no longer deserves the respect or because people are rejecting authority due to their own egos?"

"Both."

"This is not good. You're painting a very ugly picture here."

"We? We are only showing people the picture *they've* painted. *We* are placing it on *exhibition* for all to see. And yes, it is indeed an ugly one, abstract, dark, and distorted. Yet paintings can always be reworked — painted over. This is why our message is so very critical and comes at this time. . .people have the power to change and alter the current picture. Each individual has the power to improve the scene and make it beautiful. I've come to define that which needs alteration."

"This is very depressing, you know."

"We know, but then we did not make it so. Look at the children of today who have a greater sense of self than a generation ago. They test their wings of independence at a much younger age, therefore bringing defiance and disrespect into the family life sooner than in times past. We see parents who are fearful of disciplining their errant children because those children can so easily run to the authorities with a false cry of abuse, yet children are verbally and physically abusing their parents at an alarming rate. We hear a new cry from children rise up, a demand that says: 'I *deserve*. Give me this and give me that and. . .don't tell me what to do!' Parental sacrifices are no longer recognized or appreciated because the children are obsessed with ego; food, clothing, shelter, medical care, support, and love, these are no longer enough for them. Parental *guidance* is seen as 'telling them what to do,' parental *concern* is seen as 'interference.' Well," he seemed to hesitate, "*you* know what I'm talking about here."

I didn't comment.

"Let's continue then," he said, respecting my desire to close the subject. "You would think that everyone on this planet would instinctively know that it's wrong — against God's law — to kill another. However horrifying, that's not the case."

Thou shalt not kill.

"Life has lost its sacredness. Respect for it is waning. People are seen as being expendable. On a grand scale we have observed this to be so." He sighed heavily, then in a soft yet weighted voice, "people *are killing* people. . .killing! And even the very words of that statement have lost their gravity — their absolute horror. Murder has become such a commonplace occurrence that it's evolved into an accepted fact of daily life. It's gotten so bad that children are killing children. Again, the ego is the culprit who wants the 'I' recognized as possessing power. This alleged power is thought to come by being a gang member. This ego is believed to be enhanced by wearing name brands, hence the killing for a specific type of shoe or jacket. The status of Self has become more important than *life* itself and this is a great heart pain for us to witness. Cruelty of physical abuse has oftentimes resulted in murder."

"What of self-defense?"

"We're not talking about self-defense. One has an obligation to protect and defend her or his own life. We're talking about out-and-out murder and the lack of conscience or guilt."

"What about self-defense of country? Of a whole people?"

"Only if one is attacked and then it's between weapon-wielding soldiers."

He'd read my mind. He'd seen the sickening visual I'd had of the billowing mushroom cloud fan out over Nagasaki.

He commented. "Hiroshima was a great sorrow for God. . .all of us. It was an example of how knowledge, even intellectual brilliance, is used without the wisdom that needs to accompany it. The United States was wrong to murder innocent civilians — women, children, babies, the elderly and infirm — in order to prove military superiority. In military self-defense, soldiers square against soldiers, pilots fly against pilots, ships against ships. And this principle clarifies the basic premise of nuclear weapons being an abomination to God and all the life the Mother/Father created. Earthly Spirituality declines in direct proportion to its rising technology and that imbalance will lead to nowhere other than annihilation of the human species.

"We observe the evidence of the children following in the adult's footsteps. The military machines of nations over the globe race for possession of the ultimate weapon to prove their power and, the child, desiring that same self-aggrandizing power, conceals the manly gun in the pocket of his small worn pants. The big, bad little boy with his big, bad gun reflects his big, bad country with its big, bad weapons.

"You see?" he said, "Power has been misdefined in this world. Humans believe power to be synonymous with strongest, dominant, biggest, richest, best-of-the-best, therefore these razzle-dazzle elements blind them to the *real* power — that of spiritual simplicity and wisdom.

"The fact that younger and younger children are becoming murderers is the fault of the adult society that failed to instill the correct and true meaning of power. Spartans are being raised instead of intellectuals and peacemakers. This violent planet is continuing to beget greater and greater depths of violence with each ensuing generation."

What could I say? These had been my own thoughts. These had been the very issues I'd shed tearful prayers over. "I fear it's gone too far," I whispered.

"Yes, it has gone too far, yet it only takes a moment to turn it around and reverse the downward spiral. The momentum can be ground to a screeching halt in one heartbeat."

"Choice. You're talking about Free Will choices everyone can make."

"Yes. That little boy in the dark alley can pocket his gun or turn it in, he can walk away from false power; it's his decision. All it takes is choosing what he *inherently* knows is right over what his peers coerce him to believe as the 'in' behavior."

His words caused my thoughts to apply the premise to the adult world. "The military machines also have this choice to 'turn in' their big, bad guns — destroy all their nuclear weapons, but they won't do it. They will not do it."

"Why not?"

"You and yours are far too optimistic. This is the Ego Planet, the Violent Planet, remember? This is the planet where Power is seen as Might rather than Wisdom. It's the Macho Man Planet of the Apes."

"You're getting cynical," he said with a crooked smile.

"Am I? *Am* I? I don't wear dark glasses when observing world behavior. I don't make my heart heavy for imagined reasons. I'm only responding to what I see. . .the facts. Take Hebron, for instance. Mostly Palestinians currently live there, but the Israelis want them out because the Israelis claim that that land should belong only to them. Why? Do you know why?"

"Yes, we know why. It's because the Israelis believe the roots of their religion are in Hebron."

"For *religion!*" I cried.

"Yes. And they believe the Father of their religion, Abraham, rests there."

"A *messenger!*" came my clarification. "Why, that'd be like all the American Indians demanding their original lands back because that's where their religious and cultural roots are. That'd be like Christians demanding land rights to Bethlehem because Jesus was born there. Are people *never* going to stop revering the messenger as God? Are people *never* going to realize the *roots* of spirituality and the very *Essence* of the One God lives within their own *souls*? Are they *never* going to stop bowing and kneeling to the mere human messenger or some designated soil? Do you know how spiritually primitive that sounds? They're *idolizing* humans and land. Then *killing* people over sole possession of their idol." I sighed, heavily. "These people," I moaned, "they don't understand about God nor do they know where God is found. They rip and tear at what they misinterpret as God's Pieces. They burn votive candles to imagined images reflected on buildings; they devour books by authors claiming to talk to the Virgin Mother or God when it's only the author's ego talking. I'm so in despair over the blatant and blasphemous behavior of this world. Everything and everyone has become someone's golden calf. . .even a calf."

"Yes," came the equally despair-filled voice, "and it wasn't even the calf that was originally important, nor the messenger who brought the words on her lips, it was the Word Itself. So now they revere the calf and bring it gifts of honor and sacredness."

"God's become lost among the idols," I said. "Every John Doe can make a mumbo-jumbo tape, give himself a guru name and, before you know it, everyone's passing it around as something from On High. Why are gurus more attractive than God? Why do they *have* to seek and seek? To me they look like a barnyard full of chickens running around headless, completely headless."

"Your visual is a little more graphic than ours, but the bottom line is perceived the same."

The puppies in my lap rearranged themselves and I gave them attention. Stroking their silky heads as they drifted back to sleep, I found my mood darkening.

"I'm done here, you realize. I've done all I can."

"Have you?" he questioned.

I merely nodded.

"Have you?"

Again I nodded.

He didn't push further.

I looked up into his brilliant blue eyes. "The Word has been given as a sweet whisper. It cannot be heard. . .can *never* be heard over the din of the roar."

"And the roar," he repeated, "is the razzle-dazzle you referred to, the spectacles people want to revere."

"Yes. As each day passes and I witness more and more blasphemous material and events, my work feels more and more futile. God and the Word are not a roar but a sweet and pure Whisper within. They're a warm and full feeling within the heart. They're a welling of complete joy and inner contentment. They're not the glitter or plastic idol. They're not a human or piece of land. They're not a reflection or a religion."

The visitor made no comment.

I remained lost in my mood.

The fire tried to give a snappy gaiety to the room yet had no such effect on either of us.

Finally I spoke. "I want to go home."

Silence.

"I want to go home," I repeated.

"We know."

"Well?"

"You're wrong."

"Wrong? About what?"

"About being done. You're not."

"If I can't be effective then I'm done. If the Word can't be heard above the roar then I'm done. I can't compete with the glitter."

"You have no idea who you've already touched. They needed no glitter, no roar, no miracles."

"You don't understand," I cried, "you're not down here all the time to hear that roar in your ears and see the dazzle people crave."

"You're still not seeing. . ."

"Stop it. Stop it! *Stop* it! I cannot compete with *God* down here!"

He smiled softly. He crossed the space between us to kneel before me and take my hand in his. "You're not competing with *God*, you're competing with the little *glitter* god — the blasphemous god of some authors' imagination. You need to realize that."

I appreciated his attempt. "But don't you see? It's because I *do* realize. And that realization makes so much seem futile to me. If people *think* a 'talk' with God is real, then, in relation to *their* belief, I am in competition. It's *their* viewpoint that makes it so."

"And you think they're too ignorant to discern the difference."

"No," I corrected, "I can only go by what I see them scrambling for. I can only accept what I see happening in the world. *They* decide ignorance or wisdom. *They* choose glitter or God."

"Then let them choose, Mary. *You* provide the choice. Look," he said while rising and beginning to pace before me, "this time it has to be done by one's spirit recognition instead of the dazzle that was historically utilized. Their proof of Truth has to be verified from the source within them, not a miracle-working outside source. Mary," he said, passing before me, "the cycle has got to be broken, they've got to revere the *Word* instead of the messenger this time." Our eyes locked. "You cannot count the numbers of those who hear the whispered Word, for they cherish it in a quiet, sacred way. You cannot expect to see the resulting acceptance of the whispered Word because it's as a warm and strong undercurrent of spring water. The roar and glitter that is physical and evident in a more public manner will not, *cannot* compare to the spiritual depth of the sweet silence that lies within those who choose otherwise. You are here dealing with the physical, therefore you are feeling smothered by the visual, the audible. Yet we see into the multitudes of souls who do recognize the glitter for what it is and thereby have chosen the sweet whispers to hold as their truth. Don't forget," he reminded, "you're not here to witness or gauge results, only to renew the *presentation*. We'll all watch now to see what is done with it."

I thought on the wisdom of his words. Had I been wanting to see more visible signs of people's acceptance? Had I not realized that the real numbers of those accepting God's Word would not be publicly evidenced, that it would be a privately held sacredness? Had I complicated my primary mission by expecting to see results when those weren't my responsibility?

"I serve the food," I said, "that's all I do. I think I've been waiting for the masses to partake, but that's not my role. It's the people's role to partake or not. It's all up to them."

His broad smile confirmed my words. "Yes, your eagerness has brought you undue frustration."

"But it's only natural for me to want this to be successful and. . ."

"Of course! Yes! We do too, yet you must be patient, give time for them to make recognitions, process, then make their final choice. It's very different now — the Presentation — Private Figure replaces the Public One, Undercurrent instead of Splash, the Whisper not the Roar."

I couldn't suppress a sheepish grin. "You're making me feel much better about this."

A few moments of companionable silence passed between us before I frowned, "I guess we drifted off course. Well, maybe not. We were talking about killing over land and the bodily remains of spiritual messengers, religious roots, and that brought us to idols and false beliefs. I suppose you could say we're still on track because, the way I see it, people are killing the God within them in order to embrace so many glitter gods."

"That so clearly exemplifies this Commandment's secondary intent. There're many kinds of killing."

"It doesn't sound like you're referring to hunters. Are you meaning the act of willfully killing relationships, love or trust; how people destroy so much of life's beauty?"

The archangel nodded. "That and also their environment. This destruction of life's goodness and positive aspects create a great void for the darker — negative — elements to fill up."

I was envisioning pure, sparkling water spilling out of a woodland pond while stagnant, brackish water poured in from the other side. It was a stomach-churning visual.

Observing my mental picture, he commented, "Your visualization is far more attractive than how we see the reality of it. Multiply your pond by several billion and perhaps you'll see what I mean."

My eyes closed in an effort to do just that. They shot open. "I can't."

"You can. What you mean to say is that you don't want to. You don't want to see the reality of it. . .yet you can't help *feeling* it."

I didn't comment.

"You don't have to say anything. These things you feel contribute to the reasons why you want to go home, do they not?"

Silence.

"More and more frequently you feel like an outlander or alien. You find it increasingly difficult to figure people's behavior and this. . ."

"Could we not talk about me?"

"I'd like to help," he softly replied.

Silence.

"May I?"

I shrugged my shoulders.

He took that as a faint green light. "I want you to know that I wasn't chastising you. We know you feel the things we do and, being down here, you also feel a weight that we do not. This weight makes you yearn for the lightness of the Home you remember; however, it is that same weight that reminds you of why you're here and that we never stop trying. We keep plugging along, renewing and reviving the message."

"But things are so much worse here now."

"And so our message corresponds — it's stronger. Our message comes as a mirror to reflect people's behavior. It says: Look upon yourselves and see how your words, thoughts, and actions are closing the Light out of your lives.

See how your negativity and ego-centered attitudes are lowering the collective consciousness of humankind. *Change* before you self-destruct!"

"Change," I echoed. "As simple as making a choice." But, I thought, *did* people want to change? Had they become comfortable in their negativity, their grumping and complaining? I couldn't believe that. A smile felt so much better than a frown, the uplifting feel of joy was so much more enjoyable than the heaviness of depression and continual states of negativity. The archangel had reached the Fifth Commandment, there was more to his message. "Let's keep going," I suggested.

He smiled. "We want to make this mirror as clear as we can for people, no room for misinterpretation, no room for excuses. If we can help them to turn their behavior around, they'll realize potential they never knew they had. Most of all, they'll finally be a joy to God instead of a sorrow.

"Now, we were discussing the different kinds of killing. Beside the obvious physical kind we've observed a great increase in behavioral killing. Out of jealousy, friendships are killed. A controlling, manipulative personality destroys family relationships. Desire for power smothers all in its path. Superiority kills respect. Prejudice kills brotherly love. Gossip kills trust. Slander kills reputation. Ego destroys all."

"Negativity," I said, "really does seem to be an epidemic. There are so many little elements in one's life that can brighten a day, yet these aren't even seen much less appreciated. People are too caught up in themselves to look elsewhere, around them." My gaze lowered to the puppies in my lap. "These little ones give me such joy. They make me feel loved, they bring big smiles to my face and make me laugh. I'm so thankful for them. They accept me for me; no jealousy, no judgments, no assumptions or expectations. . .just love."

"Precisely. Just love. And that begins to flow forth when people accept others in an unconditional manner. No gossip, no judgments, no expectations or assumptions."

He'd paused long enough for me to take a moment to check on the fire. I eased the sleeping pups down onto the seat and rose from the chair. The fire flames still danced over the same logs I'd put in just before my meditation had begun. I didn't question the oddity and returned to my chair without comment.

"Loyalty, too, has lost meaning. Loyalty and fidelity," he said. "Love and commitment."

Thou shalt not commit adultery, I thought.

"And yes, now we have moved to the Sixth Commandment which concerns loyalty and fidelity and commitment; of which little is evidenced in this current world."

This issue made me somewhat nervous. I was healing and hoped he wouldn't bring personal experiences into this subject. Rather than voicing my thought, I listened.

"The obvious, in regard to this Commandment, would correlate to marriage, of course.
It's a given, is it not? It's a given that married
partners remain loyal and faithful to one another, committed to their love. They support
each other in all ways. They do not focus
on Self. Everything is done for the good of
the pair, never for the one, yet all the while,
respecting each other's beautiful individuality
and giving each other the freedom to express
and experience that unique individuality. Marriage is exhibiting a respect for the other's
uniqueness. Marriage is never an 'I,' it is a
coexistence of a 'We;' a wonderful coexistence.
Yet some would perceive it as a *blend* and
that's when trouble starts. Two uniquely different individuals should never expect, or wish,
to blend, for then one will expect — often
demand — the other to give up her uniqueness.
Is this not adultery?"

I frowned at the new idea. "You're saying
that the *ego* is the mistress in that case."

He made an affirmative gesture.

"Mmm, I never thought of it that way before."

"Few have."

"Well. . .well no wonder I had such a hard
time trying to figure things out," I mumbled.

"Pardon me? I didn't get what you said."

"Nothing," I replied, resisting the urge to think
about the *double*-blow from which I'd been healing.
"So adultery can refer to any element that one
mate prioritizes over the love for his partner?"

"That's too light," he advised. "Let us use the word *impassioned* instead of prioritize."

"But married people, in their unique individuality, can be impassioned over all kinds of outside aspects, issues, goals, etc."

His brow rose then, "To the depth, to the point, of consumption? To the point of no return where nothing, no *one* is important any more? To the point where the love of one's partner isn't even seen, much less felt?"

"Well. . ." now I understood exactly what he meant. "How does love just go away? I mean, if two people *really* love each other, how is it possible to have something or someone else become *greater* than that love?"

"That I cannot answer."

"How can I understand this if *you* can't explain it for me?"

"Because the reasons are too varied and you wish to keep this on a general basis. Mary, the common denominator for adultery is ego. Whether it be a desire for success or personal attention, whether it be for individual status or for sexual reasons makes no difference. The point of it is this: the 'We' of the marriage suddenly becomes an 'I.' Then that 'I' makes more demands, finds new reasons to criticize the partner, becomes overly possessive, looks for excuses to place blame in order to justify actions of self. It becomes a downward spiral into darkness that can rarely be stopped. Depending on the type of mistress, different behavioral elements come into play, even violence. Yet the multitude of psychological ploys applied can all be traced back to the ego being the instigator."

"Then what makes the ego suddenly become so dominant in one's life? You don't just wake up one morning and decide Self is more important than the love for your mate!"

"No? I'm afraid that that's exactly what can and does happen."

"But why?"

"We're going in circles now. This happens for a variety of reasons depending on the individual and what represents the mistress."

"So the other mate is just tossed aside. . .just like that."

"Frequently this is how it would appear."

"Appear? Appear!"

"Do you wish this to get personal? We can go into a specific case, if you like."

"No, no I don't want to get personal. You came to give a message for the people, let's keep it to that."

"All right then, we see ego as the culprit for adultery. In a marriage it's vitally important to, at all times, maintain the perspective of *two* individuals who have a special *commitment* to one another through *love* of one another. *Two* separate, unique individuals. That's very important to never lose sight of. These two are *not* united as one individual, but as a *pair* — together, yet recognized and respected individuals. Each must respect the other's individuality without resentment or jealousy, without ridicule, restrictions, demands, or personal insecurity. When the love for each other is stronger than all else, a mate's individuality is also loved. . .and *nothing* can take priority over it. And when that condition exists, nothing can become a mistress."

"Then what you're saying is that this mistress, in a form of whoever or whatever, *couldn't* become a reality unless a mate's love has begun to wane. Is that what you're saying?"

He was almost reluctant to respond. "Yes, when the love is no longer the strongest force in one's life, another element replaces that priority position."

"I see. Now I understand."

"I'm sorry," he whispered.

Though I'd said I understood, I really didn't. How did the depth of a true love become shallow? How did its sunlight become nothing but a pinpoint? How *could* it just not be there? The archangel's voice brought my attention back to where it belonged.

"Just as ego and adultery steal away the love in a marriage, the act of stealing is manifested through a multitude of means.

Thou shalt not steal.

"The Seventh Commandment is a law that not only pertains to the material possessions of another, but also to other aspects of life as well. This law holds true for anything that can be taken from another."

The archangel seated himself across from me again and Punkin had decided to try out his lap. She licked his fingers while he gently stroked her and continued talking.

"Normally," he said, "people tend to associate the Seventh Commandment with robbery of tangible goods, yet there is all manner of robbery committed. A merchant's over-pricing is a form of stealing. Overtaxing by a government is stealing, as is forgery. Taking another's idea and claiming it as one's own is stealing. You see the widespread ramifications this issue has?"

I did. "A reputation can be stolen too. Trust and love. Well, I can see that there's nearly endless possibilities to this. Someone could steal another's job, of course that would have to be done knowingly — with willful intention — in order to be a wrongful act. Stealing can be done by way of behavior as much as actually taking something with the hands."

"This is so and, again, ego is most often the instigating force behind it."

I was pensive. "Through ego, The Way of the Word has been lost."

"I'm here to shed light on The Way. As you've said, The Way has been paled by the plastic razzle-dazzle. We felt an extreme urgency to illumine The Way once more, emphasize its beautiful simplicity."

"The Way is as simple as adhering to the Ten Commandments, yet people view that as being too simple. They think there must be more to. . ."

"If it is so simplistic," he interjected, "why is it that we find their collective consciousness vibrating at such a dangerously low and dark frequency?"

"Well that's just it, isn't it. I agree with you and ask the same question of myself. Many times over I've asked this and tried to understand. They seek ways of spiritual complexity and esoteric knowledge, yet can't seem to follow the most basic laws of The Way. If I told them that all they ever had to do was to follow the Ten Commandments, that those *are* The Way, they'd laugh at me."

"Would they laugh at me also? At my message from the Most High? Do you think so?"

Silence.

"Mary?"

I didn't reply.

"Do you really believe they are that far gone?"

"You and yours would know this better than I."

"You're hedging. What do you think will be their response?"

"I can't answer that. I can't answer that because I don't know what their response will be. They're like lost lambs accepting shelter from every strange shepherd who happens across their path — every shepherd but The Shepherd. They've lost personal recognition of God. They've lost their way of The Way."

"Then you don't think our message will be taken to heart? You don't think it will be recognized? *Enough* for them?"

"I didn't say that, not really. I only stated the facts of their behavior that we've both observed. But they also have the luxury of choice. They can continue seeking out and chasing after the esoteric, the false shepherds, or they can turn in their tracks to follow the simplistic beauty of The Way. Who knows. What I think isn't germane, it's what *they'll* think that matters. It's what they choose to *do* that matters."

He smiled. "I'm glad to see you aren't taking personal responsibility for the results that others must determine."

"Their free will choices aren't mine to make. I've learned something from this discourse. It's not that I believe they're 'that far gone,' but perhaps their vision has been handicapped by the blinding glare of the dazzle. We'll see."

"Let's pray that isn't so, and yes, we'll wait and watch. Meanwhile, we were discussing the Seventh Commandment and the importance of making specific realizations and associations with it. People need to understand the many and varied methods of stealing that can be committed throughout their lives. Cheating is stealing, even if it's cheating on a test, as that constitutes the stealing of grade points. Cheating when giving back change is stealing money. Cheating in a relationship is stealing trust, not only from the mate, but also from oneself. When one cheats by any method, he or she steals the personal traits of integrity and trustworthiness from self."

"I think we could come up with a week's worth of ways to steal, to go against the Seventh Commandment," I said. "You've certainly made the point clear enough to me, I don't think anyone's going to have any trouble recognizing the individual ways they may or may not be guilty of regarding this issue."

"Nor I. Let's move on. Now, earlier, you gave examples of what could be stolen. You mentioned reputation, trust, and love. Reputation and trust are stolen through gossip and slander."

Thou shalt not bear false witness against thy neighbor. He had eased into the Eighth Commandment by picking up a thread from the Seventh. I listened as he spoke.

"Do you know why people gossip?"

His question threw me off guard. "I could probably come up with an acceptable answer, but my problem is that I can't figure it — I can't understand the *why* of it. I mean. . ."

"You *intellectually* know the why of it, however, you can't *spiritually* comprehend the why of it."

"Yes!" I brightened, "That's right! I *know* why they do it but I don't know why it seems so *important* to do it. It's such a total waste of energy and valuable communication time. Everywhere I go I hear gossip of some type. Everyone is talking about someone. It's become a national pastime and I wonder where good, intellectual discourse has gone. And why is it anyone's business what other people are doing anyway? Seems to me if people stopped minding other folks' business and focussed more on their own lives things would be a lot better right now."

"That's a given," he said.

I didn't comment further. My thoughts were drifting.

He'd read them. "Time to get personal?" he queried.

I looked him in the eye. "No." Then, "well. . .I don't know, it's just so sad, that's all."

"What's sad?"

"You know, this whole gossip thing."

"If it helps any, you'll recall that the same sort of thing was rumored of Jesus in his time."

Silence.

"Mary, we foresaw where your future was headed. You required someone to take over as supporter, companion, and helper. You needed an assistant, a liaison to handle your worldly business. We took care of that and sent that person to you. Just because your helper is a woman shouldn't have to infer you've changed your lifestyle."

"Evidently *that's* not a given to some people," I said. "Sometimes I feel like you sent me a real angel because she helps me in so many ways; takes care of so many of the worldly aspects in my life, is the only person I can really talk to on a high philosophical and spiritual level, be my sounding board." I grinned. "How was it that you sent a near-clone anyway? I've lost count of the times we begin to say the same things at the same time. We even catch ourselves *thinking* the same."

His smile broadened into a beaming light. "You know the answer to that. Your pasts have been closely intertwined. We could make no more appropriate choice for you."

I thought back through time to an age two thousand years ago when a woman named Mary gave up her own independent lifestyle to become my life helper and companion after my husband took off for a more interesting life in Egypt. The parallels were nearly identical. Other lives played through my mind. When I again locked eyes with my visitor, his expression had turned solemn.

"Rumors are generated from ignorance," he whispered, "and it is ignorance that keep them going."

"Oh, I know that. It's not for myself that I feel bad. . .I mean. . .well. . ." I sighed. "I need to start over here. I have a friend who owns a bookstore and she told me that a woman came into the store to announce that she wasn't buying any more of my books because she'd *heard* I'd changed my lifestyle."

"How did you feel about that revelation?"

"Well, initially, I was shocked regarding the *subject* matter of the rumor, but then I felt really sad, sad because this woman so readily and unconditionally *believed* this false rumor. I felt so sad for her because she didn't even take personal responsibility for that which she so automatically *accepted* as truth. That's what bothered me most because people who really know me would defend the truth and set those rumors straight." I paused just long enough for him to comment without seeming to interrupt me.

"We see a preponderance of surface thought throughout the world."

"It's not just surface thought that gossip involves, is it. It's a serious lack of personal responsibility too, maybe even more so. I've given much thought to this silly rumor about me and, well, what if the helper you sent me had been a male? What sordid rumors would fly from that situation? A sexual one, right?"

"Most probably so."

"Well, the way I see it, this 'changed lifestyle' thing only started because this is such a sexually-based culture where absolutely *everything* has to have some sort of sexual connotation. What of nuns in a convent? What of the twelve apostles — all men — leaving wives and families to follow and live with Jesus? Where has the fact of platonic relationships gone to? The sexual fascination and preoccupation of peoples' minds is a personal grief to me. It's as if people can't believe someone could be celibate, much less choose to be. Have these people become so sexually inebriated that they cannot conceive of a purely companionable relationship?"

"It would appear to be so. You'll find no argument here, for what you say is true. We've already established that this is a physically-based planet, hence the negativity and violence that comes by way of an ego-focused society. Your own experience with this Commandment clearly indicates how far-reaching this concern of ours is."

"It's far reaching alright, that's pretty obvious, yet I don't understand why people would want to behave in such a shallow manner."

"They don't see it that way — as shallow thought — because they don't *apply* thought."

"What's going to turn things around?" I asked with a heavy sigh. "What's going to bring real spiritual substance to the world?"

"We're hoping a good, long look in our mirror will accomplish that."

"Uh-huh. You bring a last message — your mirror — and expect results by what people see of themselves. I brought fresh water and expected them to drink. What's the difference?"

His brow rose. "Don't you know?"

Silence.

He patiently waited for my answer.

I blushed. "Yeah, I know. I was taking it *personal.* I was personally taking responsibility for good results. It's up to them."

He winked. "You got it."

"So getting back to gossip," I said, "I know it persists because of negative or base emotions, like jealousy, prurient interests, prejudice, fear, revenge, self-aggrandizement, etc., but the real issue is integrity, isn't it? One loses one's own integrity through gossip. Through gossip one broadcasts to others that he or she cannot intellectually recognize the truth, that is," I clarified, "if the rumor is false. Gossip advertises one's lack of personal responsibility and maturity. It says, 'I have knowledge of this rumor but not the wisdom to check it out.' It reveals someone who makes assumptions and jumps to unsubstantiated conclusions."

"Yes, the real issue is personal integrity and respect for others, an inability to *accept* others, an accentuation and perpetuation of the negative."

"Not all rumors are negative, though," I added. "But even so, there is still the responsibility to insure their rightness."

"Our message for this Commandment is that gossip and slander kill the reputation of others and the integrity of self." He paused to look down at the pup asleep in his lap. After giving her a few gentle strokes across her back, he said, "the Ninth Commandment, **Thou shalt not covet thy neighbor's wife**, refers to lust; and the Tenth Commandment, **Thou shalt not covet thy neighbor's goods**, refers to envy and greed. . .both Commandments having the common denominator of possessiveness. Lust equates to the sexual prevalence on earth, how it permeates all elements of society. Envy and greed are the waste by-products of ego, the possessiveness of continual wanting, having, and the all-important goal of the getting. Physical pleasures and personal possessions are the goals of earthly humanity. This we have observed. This is what needs to be reversed.

"Presently, and as has been the case throughout history, humankind has been self-serving. It is because of this behavior that prejudice and racism still exist today. The focus on self needs to be broadened to encompass, not only all of humanity, but also all living beings."

"The animal kingdom too," I said.

"Of course. When there is recognition and respect for *all* life, the priority of Self falls by the wayside because then one understands the interconnectedness of all living beings. Then one understands that one species is interdependent upon the other in some vital way. Life is like a fragile yet strong web woven to connect the many thriving elements together."

"Visually that brings to mind the beautiful living web of the American Indian's Grandmother Spider," I commented.

"Precisely. And within that living Web is not only earthly human, animal, and plant life, but also the entwined life of Beings everywhere."

I smiled at that. "You're referring to our Starborn family, life on other planets. We're really a neighborhood, aren't we, just one big sky neighborhood."

A twinkle sparkled from his eye. "And you're going to teach the children that, aren't you."

"Yes," I admitted, "I've already written the book. It's a very basic and simple picture book. I thought it best to begin with the basic fact that earth is but one neighborhood in a universe full of many neighborhoods, that we are all connected and that there's no such thing as an alien being. I wanted to reach the smallest children with this so they wouldn't grow up without knowing their true heritage. I called it *Star Babies* and my friend is doing the illustrations for it."

"Your timing is precise for this. Your work will become more public in 1998."

"The children's book will come out in the fall of '97," I corrected.

He became solemn, "In '98 it will become more public," he repeated.

I didn't comment further or ask what he meant.

"Mary, when you say 'Starborn,' who is it you're referring to, exactly?"

"I'm referring to intelligent beings everywhere," I said, spreading my arms in a wide stretch, "out there in our universal neighborhood and here on earth. We too are Starborn. The Web of Life is woven in such a way as to catch all the planets upon the fine threads. We are all beautiful beings, all children of the one God who created us all. There's no such thing as an alien being, only neighbors we've yet to meet."

"A friendly way to put it."

"Well, isn't it so?"

"It is so," he nodded, "yet the neighbors of earth must also realize that there have been visits and interaction from their other planetary neighbors."

"I think that idea is finally getting through."

"And that that interaction, through various ways, has been ongoing, also since the beginning of time."

"I think that's just starting to sink in and, when that's really understood, their idea of the Starborn people being like gods will finally diminish. We're all people with different levels of spiritual and technical advancement."

"Yes. Just as on earth you have people building space shuttles in one region and people building weaving shuttles in other regions, so too are the vast differences of planetary neighborhoods in the universe. Is this not what your *Star Babies* book reveals for children?"

I grinned at his reference to the book. "Reveals? I don't see it as a revelation for children, just a way to help them grow up with knowledge of reality instead of being only exposed to violent, monster-type alien movies. They need truth, not misconceptions born of earthly fear, speculation, and fantasy. After all, we've had interplanetary DNA for a long, long time and that fact is long overdue to come to light."

"Other facts need to see the light also. It is time."

"I think so too. For a long while I was reluctant because of how I thought people would react and rebel, deny and balk. Maybe I've just grown into a certain serenity over it. Now I'm of the mind that truth, no matter how contrary it may seem to current, popular belief systems, is always wisest. I've grown into a surety that people shouldn't be kept in an adult tooth fairy belief system. It's time they were told that there's no Santa Claus. It's time

they understood that most all their religious leaders and messengers were their star neighbors
come to show The Way." I paused to gather
my thoughts. "Maybe if they really understand
this then they'll see how childlike it was to
make religions out of the different messengers'
words and make gods of the messengers. Different spiritual messengers for different cultures
of people, yet all messengers representing the
one God on High who the people ended up
splintering into many."

"Our message," he said, "is for people to think
universally. One God of earth. That same one
God of the universe. All children of the one
God. Jesus, physically conceived of Starborn seed
through their medical technology (artificial in-
semination) and born under their ball of light —
your Christmas Star — that led the Magi onward,
is only one example of their efforts to bring
truth to those on earth. The so-called miracles
of the bible were no more than the workings
of higher physics that could not be understood,
explained or even grasped at the time. Starborn
technology created the Christmas Star, the Burning Bush, the pharaoh's plagues, voices in the
clouds, apparitions of religious figures. Their technology was the ships interpreted as flaming char-
iots. Their holographic images were seen as
apparitions from heaven. The parting of the Red
Sea was their handiwork, as was simple levitation
perceived as walking-on-water. These few examples were those that were applied solely because

the people of earth required dazzle in order to believe."

"Yes but then they made religions of the dazzle and gods of the dazzler. Can you tell me why our star neighbors didn't just forego all their technical displays and opt for reality instead?"

"You can answer that. Think about it a bit. Put yourself back to biblical times and before. Go ahead, I'll wait."

Thinking.

Waiting.

"They would've made gods of the new visitors. In fact they did, didn't they? Some of the Egyptian gods and goddesses were designed after some of the star people. In fact," I added, "so are some of the American Indian kachinas. Some of the kachinas closely resemble the binature physiology of the Egyptian gods and goddesses. It was the Starborn's physical influence that made the building of the pyramids possible, through levitation — antigravitational means. But. . .if the reality of other planets and beings populating them was *explained* back then. . ."

"Go deeper with your thought," he advised.

Thinking.

Waiting.

"They'd want the Starborn's advanced technology. They'd want to possess knowledge and technology they weren't ready for. That's why Atlantis is gone, and Lemuria. Earthly humanity needed to naturally evolve and make their own discoveries at the proper and corresponding pace — consecutively, sequentially. Their advancements had to be aligned with their spiritual and intellectual development. . .wisdom."

"You have the general idea, still. . .look what was done in your so-called modern times with the atom bomb. Earthly wisdom is still not aligned with the advancement of its own technology. Look at where nuclear power went — into missiles to annihilate the entire planet, destroy all life! And so! Our message is to stop revering the ego of Self! See life as *all* living things. Expand your field of vision, beyond your world of self. Realize the interconnectedness of all living things. One God equals one Way — the Ten Commandments — The *Way*, nothing more complex, esoteric or dogmatic than that. Understand Unconditional Love, really understand it and *live* it, *feel* it. Respect one another and all living things, and here now is my prophecy, for *if you do not turn your current behavior around, your continued selfishness and negativity will destroy your world. It is your own negative behavior that will bring you down. Earthly humanity could die by its own hand.*"

A shiver trembled through me. "That's not even a warning, that's a fact, isn't it."

"It's a prophetic statement with zero probability for change. It's why we've felt such deep concern, such urgency to bring the Word one final time. The Apocalypse of Revelations is not a physical event, but an event within each individual. The transformation is personal, from *within*. And what transpires within is transferred to the without. Change from within and there will be a changed world also. It is time."

"Time. . ." I began to wonder aloud.

"Time? Is there time to halt the spinning downward spiral that humankind has generated? You tell me."

How could I answer that? Then, "Choice. All it takes is each person making a committed choice to practice unconditional love and bury their self-centeredness."

He was so solemn. "Yes. . .it is all up to them. They brought their world to what it is today, they can continue their current behavior and annihilate it or they can bring it back into beauty. . .it's all a matter of making a personal choice. . .one simple choice."

It sounded as though we were headed toward turning earth into a Sodom and Gomorrah yet had one final opportunity to create a paradise of it. Seeing the sadness within the archangel's eyes and heart, I couldn't imagine anyone not taking this final message, given out of love for us, as a call for personal reevaluation and action. Ultimately I saw his message as the elusive Hope we've all been grasping so desperately for. There *was* hope after all. . .and only *we* have the power to strengthen it, only *we* have the power to make it a living force in our lives. And all we have to do to make it manifest is follow the Ten Commandments — The Way. All we have to do is make one choice. The outcome is in nobody's hands but ours.

I awoke in my chair. Pinecone was curled up in my lap. The woodstove was cold. There was no sign of my visitor. I stretched and raked shaking fingers through my hair. What had just happened? Had I fallen asleep after my meditation and dreamed it all? Had the beautiful man of light — the archangel — come in my dream?

I rested back in the chair and calmly looked about the room. Punkin was sound asleep right where the archangel's lap had been and there was a perceptible quality to the room that I couldn't quite define. It shifted between a sorrowful weight-bearing heaviness and a springy lightness that almost made me want to giggle with joy. In my mind I recalled the visual image of my visitor sitting across from me. His manifested beingness had left my cabin, his beingness had vanished, but not his sorrow. . .nor his hope.

SIX MONTHS LATER

Though I'd planned to take time off from writing, the archangel's message made that an impossibility. The day after his visit, I called Bob Friedman at Hampton Roads and advised him of my plan to release *The Visitation* in the spring of 1997. I then surprised him with two additional books for the fall of that same year. *Star Babies*, a children's picture book that'd been on my mind for quite some time. Even though it may be controversial, the timing for it was at hand and I could no longer question its rightness. The idea for the second fall release was born of my conversation with the archangel. He'd said I'd find a way for folks to realize and count their daily blessings and I did. . .a personal blank journal to write in. *Millennium Memories* will cover three years of daily experiences with an allotted space at the end of each week to recall and count one's blessings that were given or received. So, instead of doing no books in 1997, I ended up with three. Such is the way of an archangel's influence.

Now, if I may, I'd like to express some personal thoughts related to the archangel's message. What was most striking to me was the fact that he presented *The Way* on a silver platter! I would think that millions of formerly-frustrated seekers will be overjoyed to now know that all they have to do to live a spiritually-fulfilled life is adhere to the Ten Commandments as best they can. How much easier could it be? No more wondering. No more looking about here and there. No more seeking this or that. No more complex philosophies to unravel or decipher. Goodness is the key. Goodness and unconditional love.

He spoke of changing our world by changing within. I've written a considerable amount of material regarding the issue of "going within," and I think that many people still don't really understand what this means. It doesn't necessarily pertain to meditation, although that practice will certainly bring tranquility and a calming effect to one's life. Going Within means *introspection* and *contemplation*. In terms of the archangel's reference, he means *self-evaluation* through a hard and completely honest look at your behavior; thoughts, actions, and the reasons for same. When our behavior is closely examined and we ask ourselves, "Is this how I would act in God's presence? Would my behavior please God?" then we begin to make adjustments to questionable behavior, we begin to alter it for the better. This then raises the quality of our Collective Consciousness and, as the archangel predicted, will correspondingly alter our physical world into one of restored beauty and revived hope.

I was especially pleased to hear the archangel address the subject of the Trinity by defining their (angelic) knowledge of Its true composition. He clarified the male/female balance within God's essence and dispelled the old myth generated by the male priests and religious elders of ancient times.

As Creator of all life, God would naturally have a mother aspect to balance the father qualities. God is totality; therefore, God is All That Is, including both genders. . .Mother/Father. God possesses the more stringent aspects of a demanding father and also the compassionate elements of a forgiving mother. What's important for us to remember is that these two genders blend and meld to create the whole of God's Beingness and shouldn't be separated out into two individual entities in our minds. Just as we all possess the duality of both gender qualities — the yin and the yang — so too does God.

The second aspect of God's nature is the manifestation of the Male Essence within the third dimension, who is referred to as the Son. God sends the Son into the physical as a human emissary to spiritually enlighten the children of earth. The Son Aspect has always been a visible

Presence, walking among humankind, and can be known by the names of various historically-famous spiritual leaders. The purpose of the Son's repeated returns to earth was to renew The Word of God and redefine The Way back to God, yet each time He appeared, a new religion was formed in His name and this displeased God. In the end, God saw that sending His Male Aspect as an earthly human messenger was not working. It was not working because the people revered the messenger as God.

Enter the Holy Spirit, whom the angels and all the powers of light know as God's Female Aspect, or Daughter. God the Daughter works through the human soul and appeals to people's Higher Self, the inner knowing and emotional sensitivity. God the Daughter does not walk among the people making proclamations or doing miracles to attract followers. God the Daughter is the *Spirit* of the Mother/Father at work in the world. She remains unseen for the purpose of keeping The Word above the physical Self of Her beingness. God the Daughter's spiritual presence in the world has been recognized throughout time and has been given the term, Shekhinah, meaning: God's presence in the world. The Shekhinah has no religions established in Her name. She does not utilize miracles to dazzle human minds and She rejects followers, in that She rejects titles such as spiritual leader, guru, goddess, etc. When she comes in human form she does not make Herself known.

God the Son and God the Daughter are the Male and Female Aspects of God the Mother/Father at work in the world. God the Son is a touchable entity utilizing the ego and the presence of Self to renew The Word. God the Daughter is an unseen entity utilizing the Spirit and the presence of The Word to inspire a rekindling of the truth in earthly souls.

My final comment is in regard to fear, fear associated with our future, specifically the Millennium and the idea of the Apocalypse of Revelations being so commonly associated with it.

First of all, the date of the true Millennium is not the year 2000, but rather 2001. . .the *end* of 2000 marks the first year of the Millennium's actual *birth* count. Just as a baby is not one year old at birth, neither is the Millennium a countable year until the start of 2001. This also has to do with the lack of a symbol for zero in the ancient Roman numerical system which, consequently, began the counting of the Current Era (formerly A.D.) one year *after* Christ's birth. That fact alone sets the true Millennium date *forward* to 2001.

Now there have been other Millenniums throughout history and we are all still here. I would be extremely reluctant to view this one as being any different or fear its approach. The end of the world is not upon us. Didn't the archangel say there was time to turn things around. . .if choices were made now? There will always be doomsday sayers and there will always be powerful forces of nature at work on our planet; one incites fear, the other asks for indulgence. The natural geological elements of our planet are always in continual motion by way of active and reactive forces because Grandmother Earth is a living, breathing entity — always expanding and contracting, always responding in direct correlation to human behavior. These natural movements do not necessarily evidence a doomsday effect.

The End Times have been with us for years. Revelations — the Apocalypse — is purely symbolic. It is a *transformation* that takes place *within* us. The Four Horsemen have been concurrently riding through our twentieth century and who of you have looked up to recognize any one of them as they passed by? The Apocalypse is a *personal* event that transpires within each of us. It is a personal transformation. One that comes from one's personal recognition of spiritual revelations within self.

We need to look forward to our future, not fear it. We need to follow The Way and restore earth's beauty as we restore our own. We need to gaze into the crystal spring water and see ourselves as a reflection of God's love. We need to rekindle the flame of hope in our hearts and walk forth with the light of God within our souls because. . .only *we* can heal our world, only we can return God's smile.

Books by Mary Summer Rain

Since 1985, when **Spirit Song** *first appeared, uncounted thousands have discovered Mary Summer Rain and "No-Eyes," the wise old Native American woman who taught the young Mary Summer Rain many things. The following books have been written and published:*

Spirit Song: The Visionary Wisdom of No-Eyes (1985), relates how the two first met. Although totally blind from birth, No-Eyes lived on the land, identifying everything she needed by smell and touch. Using gentle discipline, humor, and insight, she guided Summer Rain through a remarkable series of experiences, giving her the accumulated knowledge of her own eight decades.

Phoenix Rising: No-Eyes' Vision of the Changes to Come (1987), used the analogy of the phoenix, the mythical bird that symbolizes rebirth and eternal life, to provide a powerful warning of the earth changes in store for us. This unforgettable prophecy has already begun to come true, as the daily newspaper and TV news broadcasts demonstrate.

Dreamwalker: The Path of Sacred Power (1988), is the story of No-Eyes' introduction of Mary to Brian Many Heart, who taught Mary the power of the Dreamwalker by bringing her to face some painful realities. In it, she deals with many unanswered questions about her own identity and her role in traveling the path of knowledge. One of the best spirit-walking books in print.

Phantoms Afoot: Journeys Into the Night (1989), is a fascinating description of the quiet work done by Mary and her husband Bill in liberating spirits lost between two worlds. You might call these ghost stories, but ghost stories told with concern for the welfare of the ghost! Like the previous three volumes, *Phantoms Afoot* is very much set in Colorado. All the wild beauty of the Colorado countryside enters into the story.

Earthway (1990), Mary Summer Rain's fifth book, is a presentation of the knowledge of the Native Americans. Interweaving the inspired teachings of No-Eyes with a wealth of practical knowledge of all kinds, she demonstrated a practical, gentle, *civilized* way of life. Divided into sections for body, mind and spirit, the book aimed at restoring wholeness. (Published by Pocket Books, but available from Hampton Roads.)

Daybreak: The Dawning Ember (1991), Mary's sixth book, is divided into two parts. "The Communion" consisted of extensive answers to questions she had received from readers over the years. Ranging from prophecy to Native American history, from metaphysics to just plain common sense, here were nearly 450 pages of wisdom, including an extensive section on dream interpretation.

The second section, called "The Phoenix Files," is a comprehensive collection of maps, charts, lists, and tables describing nuclear facilities, toxic-waste dumps, oil refineries, hurricane, tornado and flood-hazard zones, as well as a suggested pole-shift realignment configuration. Together, it made an indispensable resource manual.

Soul Sounds: Mourning the Tears of Truth (1992), is the book Mary's readers long waited for: her own story, in her own words, of the experiences that shaped her extraordinary life, from childhood to her most recent meetings with Starborn friends. This was her private journal, written for herself and for her children. She didn't want it published. But her advisors insisted, and finally she gave in. . .and the reader reaction has been nothing short of phenomenal.

Mountains, Meadows and Moonbeams: A Child's Spiritual Reader (1984, 1992), was originally privately printed by Mary and Bill. Only in 1992 was the first trade paperback edition made available by Hampton Roads Publishing Company. This simple, delightful, easy-to-read book is full of illustrations for coloring; it will help parents nurture the creativity and imagination of their children; and will help children to understand where we come from and who we as humans really are.

Whispered Wisdom (1993) is a collection of beautiful photographs taken by Mary Summer Rain which depict the four seasons of Colorado. It is a celebration of nature, accompanied by a collection of verse, prose, vignettes, and sayings taken from her woods-walking journal. Together the pictures and words weave a wonderful tapestry of the many faces of Mother Earth.

Ancient Echoes (1993) is a magical collection of chants, prayers, and songs of the Anasazi people, who lived in pueblos on the plateau area of the American Southwest from around 100 to 1300 A.D. Mary Summer Rain brings forth the beauty and sensitivity of the Anasazi heart by recreating many of the chants used by one Anasazi community called the Spirit Clan. The information came from "spiritual memory recall," whereby she received, in deep meditative states, both the words and the spirit of the words. These chants, prayers, and songs also have many practical uses, for healing, blessings, child sleep songs, for a broken heart. Illustrated with line drawings, it is a stunning and practical book.

The Seventh Mesa (1994) is Mary Summer Rain's first novel, though she pointedly asks the question for the reader to decide: is it *really* fiction? It's about a hidden pyramid buried beneath a Southwest mesa, and a guarded chamber that holds the sacred scrolls and tablets which reveal the answers to humanity's most puzzling mysteries through the ages. But is it time for us to discover those answers? Have we gained enough wisdom to know what to do with that information? Four interesting characters come together to take that fascinating and dangerous adventure.

Bittersweet (1995) is a continuation of the *Soul Sounds* journal, but in the format of a collection of stories, rather than a day-by-day diary. It deals with the outstanding events in Mary Summer Rain's life since 1992. Some of these events, including her interactions with her Starborn friend, are quite astounding in their implications. Illustrated with line drawings, and a twelve-page color photo section, *Bittersweet* will be one of the most informative, interesting, and controversial books for Mary Summer Rain's readers.

Mary Summer Rain on Dreams (1996) with Alex Greystone. For years readers have written Mary Summer Rain requesting interpretations of literally hundreds of their dreams. In both *Earthway* and *Daybreak*, she addressed this need, adding a short list of interpreted dream symbols. Here, in collaboration with Alex Greystone, she has created an entirely new, single-volume reference guide to more than 14,500 dream symbols. *Mary Summer Rain on Dreams* is a comprehensive dictionary of dream symbols and "key word" clues, with short, succinct, easy-to-understand interpretations. She has shared her insight into the world of spirit, giving us a powerful interpretive tool to help in our own transformative journeys.

Hampton Roads Publishing Company
publishes and distributes books on a variety of subjects,
including metaphysics, health, integrative medicine,
visionary fiction, and other related topics.

To order or receive a copy of our latest catalog, call toll-free,
(800) 766-8009, or send your name and address to:

Hampton Roads Publishing Company, Inc.
134 Burgess Lane
Charlottesville, VA 22902